THE
PRESIDENTS
OF THE UNITED STATES

THE PRESIDENTS

OF THE UNITED STATES

SIMON ADAMS

MINNETONKA, MINNESOTA

Two-Can Publishing
11571 K-Tel Drive
Minnetonka, MN 55343
www.two-canpublishing.com

Editorial Director: Jill Anderson
Editor: Charles Pederson
Cover Design: Laurie Fritsche
Project Manager: Jennifer Caliandro

Originally created for Two-Can by

Picthall & Gunzi Ltd

21A Widmore Road, Bromley, Kent BR1 1RW, England
Tel: (0)20 8460 4032 Fax: (0)20 8460 4021

Library of Congress Cataloging-in-Publication Data
Adams, Simon, 1955–
   The presidents of the United States : completely revised and updated to include the
2004 election / Simon Adams.
      p. cm.
   Summary: "Describes the role of president in the United States' government and
outlines the careers of the 43 people who have held the office"—Provided by publisher.
   Includes index.
   ISBN 1-58728-527-4 (reinforced hardcover) — ISBN 1-58728-528-2 (softcover)
1. Presidents--United States—Biography—Juvenile literature. 2. Presidents—United States—
Juvenile literature. 3. United States—Politics and government—Juvenile literature. I. Title.
   E176.1.A425 2005
   973'.09'9—dc22

1 2 3 4 5 09 08 07 06 05

Printed and bound by Tien Wah Press Pte. Ltd., Singapore
Color reproduction by All Systems Color, USA

Words in **bold** in the text can be found in the glossary at the back of the book

CONTENTS

WHAT IS A PRESIDENT?

When America won its independence from Great Britain in 1783, the leaders of the new country wrote laws on how to govern the country. These laws became the U.S. **Constitution**. U.S. leaders did not want a royal family. They decided instead that the country should be a **republic,** led by an elected head of state or president. The first president, George Washington, took office in 1789.

WHO CAN BE PRESIDENT?

The president must be at least thirty-five years old, must have been born in the United States and must have lived in the country for at least fourteen years. Both men and women may be president, but so far, the presidents have all been male. He or she cannot serve more than two terms as president, which is a total of eight years.

WHAT DOES THE PRESIDENT DO?

The president's main duty is to protect the Constitution and uphold the laws passed by **Congress.** Congress is made up of the **House of Representatives** and the **Senate**. The president can recommend new laws to Congress. The president also can veto a bill, or stop it from becoming a law, although Congress can overturn that veto with a two-thirds majority.

To help run the government, the president appoints a team called a **cabinet.** Congress must approve each cabinet member. Together, the president and the cabinet run the different **federal** departments and make sure U.S. laws, rules, and regulations are followed.

The president's administration runs the country. The Constitution limits his power through the separation of powers. The president, the court system, or **judiciary,** and Congress balance each other to make sure one does not get too powerful. But the president still has a lot of power and responsibility, including:
• serves as commander in chief of the armed forces.
• meets world leaders, appoints **ambassadors**, negotiates **treaties** and agreements, and represents America during foreign visits.
• sends new bills to Congress for approval and sets a budget, a financial plan for running the government and the country. The president influences the conduct of government by appointing officials, and acts as a symbol at times of national success or tragedy. A strong president can change the the world and make a huge impression on the lives of all Americans.

WHO IS THE VICE PRESIDENT?

From 1789–1804, the runner-up in presidential elections was appointed **vice president**. This caused great problems if the president and vice president were from different political parties. Today, the president's **running mate** becomes vice president. Part of the vice president's job is to be president of the Senate, but otherwise he or she has few formal powers. If the president dies, resigns, or is removed from office, the vice president takes over as president and appoints a new vice president.

WHERE DOES THE PRESIDENT LIVE?

The president lives at the White House, 1600 Pennsylvania Avenue, Washington, D.C. The White House serves both as a home for the president and his family and as the office of the presidency. Here, the president holds cabinet sessions and other meetings, and entertains heads of state and important visitors.

The U.S. capital is unique because it is not part of a state. It is a federal district, the District of Columbia (D.C.). It has its own mayor but no senators. It sends only one, nonvoting **delegate** to the House of Representatives.

▲The Oval Office, inside the White House, is where the president spends most of his time and makes his decisions.

ROAD TO THE WHITE HOUSE

The road to the White House is long, hard, and expensive. Candidates may enter the race more than a year before the final vote on election day. Candidates spend much of their time raising money from individuals and groups that support them. They appear on TV broadcasts and commercials and travel all over the country.

STATE BY STATE

In the months prior to the election, the states hold caucuses or primary elections. States with more people living in them have more party delegates, so candidates work hard to win support in these bigger states. Candidates try to meet as many voters as possible.

In states with caucuses, party members attend private meetings to register their votes. In states with primaries, **Republicans** and **Democrats** vote for a candidate. In primaries, winning candidates gain their state party's delegates. In caucuses, delegates don't have to vote for the winning candidate, although they usually do.

THE CONVENTION AND THE CAMPAIGN

State party delegates attend their party's national convention to vote for a candidate. The winner is the party's choice for president. At the convention, the delegates also officially nominate the candidate for vice president. The candidates again travel, hold meetings, and make speeches.

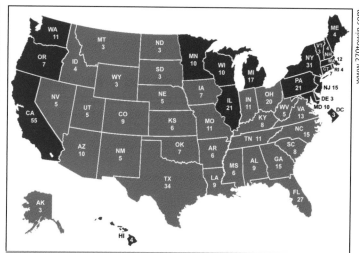

▲ Electoral votes are awarded to candidates based on the outcome of the election in each state.

▲ National political conventions are like big parties. They are intended to help excite a political party's members.

ELECTING THE PRESIDENT

On the first Tuesday after the first Monday in November, voters across America go to the polls. Each voter casts one vote, but technically, these votes don't decide the winner. The president is elected through a system known

as the **electoral college**. This group has hundreds of people called electors. Each state has electors – the same number as it has senators plus representatives. A vote for president is actually a vote for a list of state electors.

After the election, the electors meet to cast their votes for president. These votes are sent to Washington, D.C., where they are counted. Currently, the total number of electors is 538, so to win an election, a candidate needs 270 electoral votes – two more than half. Many people dislike this system because a candidate can lose the popular election yet still become president. Here's a simplified example of how that could happen:

Imagine State A has 8 million residents with eight electors. State B has 5 million residents and four electors. State C has 4 million residents and three electors. If everyone in State A votes for Mr. Republican, he receives 8 million popular votes and eight electoral votes. If everyone in States B and C votes for Ms. Democrat, she will receive 9 million popular votes. This makes her the winner of the popular vote, but she loses the election, with only seven electoral votes. Four times in U.S. history, a candidate has won the election with a minority of the popular vote.

www.270towin.com

U.S. PRESIDENTS

In more than 200 years, there have been forty-three U.S. presidents, from George Washington in 1789 to George W. Bush in 2001. So far, all of them have been men. One president, Grover Cleveland, served two separate terms. Four presidents, namely Abraham Lincoln, James Garfield, William McKinley, and John Kennedy, were assassinated in office. Another four – William Harrison, Zachary Taylor, Warren Harding, and Franklin Roosevelt – died in office. One president, Richard Nixon, was forced to resign. The ages of the presidents when they came to office range from Theodore Roosevelt at forty-two to Ronald Reagan at sixty-nine, and their terms in office from a brief thirty-two days by William Harrison to the lengthy twelve years of Franklin Roosevelt. Some, like George Washington, Abraham Lincoln, and Franklin Roosevelt, have left a powerful mark on history, while others are remembered as failures. Each one tried to govern well and has contributed to American history.

FRANKLIN PIERCE
14th president
1853–1857, Democrat
Vice President William King

MILLARD FILLMORE
13th president
1850–1853, Whig
Vice President None

ZACHARY TAYLOR
12th president
1849–1850, Whig
Vice President Millard Fillm

JAMES BUCHANAN
15th president
1857–1861, Democrat
Vice President John Breckinridge

ABRAHAM LINCOLN
16th president
1861–1865, Republican
Vice Presidents Hannibal Hamlin,
Andrew Johnson

ANDREW JOHNS
17th president
1865–1869, Demo
Vice President No

DWIGHT EISENHOWER
34th president
1953–1961, Republican
Vice President Richard Nixon

HARRY TRUMAN
33rd president
1945–1953, Democrat
Vice President Alben Barkley

FRANKLIN ROOSEVELT
32nd president
1933–1945, Democrat
Vice Presidents John Garner,
Henry Wallace, Harry Truman

HERBERT HOOVER
31st president
1929–1933, Republican
Vice President Charles Curtis

CALVIN COOLIDGE
30th president
1923–1929, Republica
Vice President Charles Da

JOHN KENNEDY
35th president
1961–1963, Democrat
Vice President Lyndon Johnson

LYNDON JOHNSON
36th president
1963–1969, Democrat
Vice President Hubert Humphrey

RICHARD NIXON
37th president
1969–1974, Republican
Vice Presidents Spiro Agnew,
Gerald Ford

GERALD FORD
38th president
1974–1977, Republican
Vice President Nelson Rockefeller

JAMES CARTER
39th president
1977–1981, Democrat
Vice President Walter Mon

GEORGE WASHINGTON
1st president
1789–1797, Federalist
President John Adams

JOHN ADAMS
2nd president
1797–1801, Federalist
Vice President Thomas Jefferson

THOMAS JEFFERSON
3rd president
1801–1809, Democratic-Republican
Vice Presidents Aaron Burr,
George Clinton

JAMES MADISON
4th president
1809–1817, Democratic-Republican
Vice Presidents George Clinton,
Elbridge Gerry

JAMES MONROE
5th president
1817–1825 Democratic-Republican
Vice President Daniel Tompkins

JAMES POLK
11th president
1845–1849, Democrat
President George Dallas

JOHN TYLER
10th president
1841–1845, Whig
Vice President None

WILLIAM HARRISON
9th president
1841, Whig
Vice President John Tyler

MARTIN VAN BUREN
8th president
1837–1841, Democrat
Vice President Richard Johnson

ANDREW JACKSON
7th president
1829–1837, Democrat
Vice Presidents John Calhoun,
Martin Van Buren

JOHN Q. ADAMS
6th president
1825–1829 Democratic-Republican
Vice President John Calhoun

ULYSSES GRANT
18th president
1869–1877, Republican
Presidents Schuyler Colfax,
Henry Wilson

RUTHERFORD HAYES
19th president
1877–1881, Republican
Vice President William Wheeler

JAMES GARFIELD
20th president
1881, Republican
Vice President Chester Arthur

CHESTER ARTHUR
21st president
1881–1885, Republican
Vice President None

GROVER CLEVELAND
22nd president
1885–1889, Democrat
Vice President Thomas Hendricks

BENJAMIN HARRISON
23rd president
1889–1893, Republican
Vice President Levi Morton

WARREN HARDING
29th president
1921–1923, Republican
President Calvin Coolidge

WOODROW WILSON
28th president
1913–1921, Democrat
Vice President Thomas Marshall

WILLIAM TAFT
27th president
1909–1913, Republican
Vice President James Sherman

THEODORE ROOSEVELT
26th president
1901–1909, Republican
Vice President Charles Fairbanks

WILLIAM McKINLEY
25th president
1897–1901, Republican
Vice Presidents Garret Hobart,
Theodore Roosevelt

GROVER CLEVELAND
24th president
1893–1897, Democrat
Vice President Adlai Stevenson

RONALD REAGAN
40th president
1981–1989, Republican
President George Bush

GEORGE BUSH
41st president
1989–1993, Republican
Vice President Dan Quayle

WILLIAM CLINTON
42nd president
1993–2001, Democrat
Vice President Al Gore

GEORGE W. BUSH
43rd president
2001–, Republican
Vice President Dick Cheney

DEATH DATES
Three of the first five presidents – Thomas Jefferson, John Adams, and James Monroe – died on July 4, Independence Day!

GEORGE WASHINGTON

GEORGE

1st president

⭐ **TERM**
1789–1797

⭐ **PARTY**
Federalist

⭐ **VICE PRESIDENT**
John Adams

⭐ **FIRST LADY**
Martha Dandridge Custis

⭐ **STATES IN THE UNION** *16*

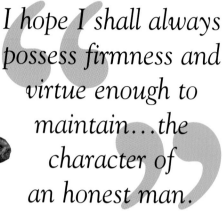

I hope I shall always possess firmness and virtue enough to maintain…the character of an honest man.

GEORGE WASHINGTON, 1788

TOOTHLESS WONDER
Washington rarely smiled in public because he had false teeth, made out of ivory and other materials.

George Washington was born into a wealthy family in Westmoreland County, Virginia, in 1732.

His father was a trader, planter, and iron mill operator, and George spent his childhood enjoying the land – hunting, fishing, riding, and boating.

▶ The birthplace of George Washington in Westmoreland County, Virginia.

EARLY LIFE
At age fifteen, Washington left school wanting to join the British Royal Navy. (Virginia was a British colony.) His widowed mother refused to let him go to sea, so he trained as a surveyor, mapping the uncharted lands to the west of Virginia. In 1753, he joined the local **militia** and fought for the British, gaining valuable experience of military life. He also became a member of the Virginia **legislature**, but he made little impression on state politics. As a farmer, he was far more interested in his estate at Mount Vernon, which he had inherited from his half brother, Lawrence.

1732
Born in Virginia

1747
Leaves school and trains as a surveyor

1753
Joins Virginia militia and fights for the British against the French

1758
Enters politics in Virginia

1761
Marries Martha Dandridge Custis, a wealthy widow

1775–1783
Revolutionary W against Britain

CROSSING THE DELAWARE

⭐ On Christmas night 1776, Washington took his 2,400 troops across the ice-bound Delaware River and surprised the German troops who were fighting for the British and were camped on the other side. His success at this battle – the Battle of Trenton – made him a national hero and helped the Americans win victory over the British in 1783.

Crossing the Delaware

INTO WAR

During the 1760s and early 1770s, relations between Great Britain and its thirteen American colonies grew steadily worse. Fighting broke out in 1775, and a year later, the colonies declared their independence. Washington, as commander in chief of the **Continental Army**, was a strong leader who inspired great loyalty among his troops. The British soldiers were successful at first, but Washington gradually won the upper hand. By 1781, the British were defeated, and by 1783, America was free.

After the war, Washington returned to his family home in Mount Vernon to farm.

In 1787, however, he was summoned to attend the **Constitutional Convention** in Philadelphia, which was putting together the constitution that would govern the new country. He was elected president of the convention, so he was the natural choice to become the first president of the United States of America in 1789.

MR. PRESIDENT

For the first four years of his presidency, Washington was busy setting up the new country. Among other things, he had to create a legal system, set **taxes**, and establish a capital city. He wanted to retire after one term, but he was persuaded to continue. War between Britain and France, attacks on U.S. shipping, and political problems at home made his last years as president unhappy.

Surprisingly, Washington was shy and modest, and he disliked public speaking and formal occasions. Although not an ambitious man, his strong sense of duty and his willingness to volunteer for public service made him a fine president. In 1797, he finally retired to his beloved Mount Vernon. When he died in 1799, George Washington, first U.S. president, was mourned across America as a brave soldier and a strong leader – truly the father of his country.

HONEST GEORGE

⭐ One story says that as a child, George Washington cut down a cherry tree on his father's farm with an axe he received as a present. He owned up with the words: "I can't tell a lie, Pa; you know I can't tell a lie." The story later was shown to be untrue.

1775
Commander in chief of the colonial army

1787
Helps write U.S. Constitution

1789
Elected first U.S. president

1792
Reelected for a second term

1797
Retires as president

1799
Dies at Mount Vernon, Virginia

▶ The Inauguration of George Washington, first president of the United States of America.

1735
Born in Braintree,
Massachusetts

1755
Graduates from
Harvard University

1758
Becomes
a lawyer

1776
Seconds the motion in
favor of independence

◀ Birthplace of John Adams
in Braintree, Massachusetts

John Adams, who was born in Braintree (now Quincy), Massachusetts, was a bright and able student. He went to Harvard University and became a lawyer, then used his knowledge of law to enter politics. Adams soon became a revolutionary and took part in anti-British campaigns. He also wrote pamphlets against the Stamp Act, a special law the British imposed on America in 1765.

The act called for taxes to be paid on legal documents, newspapers, and other printed papers.

In 1774, Adams became a member of the **Continental Congress**. He supported the **motion** in favor of independence and helped Thomas Jefferson write the Declaration of Independence. Adams also proposed that George Washington lead the Continental Army. As a result of his high profile, Adams became ambassador to France in 1777. He was not successful as a **diplomat** and in 1782 returned home, where he played an important part in negotiating the peace treaty of

☆ **TERM**
1797–1801

☆ **PARTY**
Federalist

☆ **VICE PRESIDENT**
Thomas Jefferson

☆ **FIRST LADY**
Abigail Smith

☆ **STATES IN THE UNION** *16*

2nd president

JOHN ADAMS

No man who ever held the office of president would congratulate a friend on obtaining it.

JOHN ADAMS, 1824

FAT ADAMS
John Adams ate so much that his enemies began to call him "His Rotundity," and even his wife said he was "so very fat."

◄ The French national flag, the *Tricolor*, which means three colors – red, white, and blue.

1826
Dies in Braintree, Massachusetts

1801
Loses election to Jefferson

1796
Elected president

76
ps Jefferson
te Declaration
ndependence

1777
Envoy to France and later Britain

1783
Negotiates peace treaty with Britain

1789
Elected vice president to George Washington

1783 with Great Britain. Adams spent another period of time as a diplomat, this time in Britain, but he was again unsuccessful and asked if he could return to the United States in 1788.

In 1789, President George Washington asked Adams to become his vice president. He served Washington for eight years and helped solve the arguments that broke out between the politicians of the day. When Washington stepped down as president, Adams was elected U.S. president.

THE SECOND PRESIDENT

According to the laws of the day, the candidate with the second-highest number of votes became vice president. John Adams was in the **Federalist Party**. He believed in a strong central government and by that time had become pro-Britain. His new vice president, Thomas Jefferson, was a **Democratic-Republican**, who believed in power for individual states. He was pro-France. Since Britain and France were at war with each other in Europe and since both countries were capturing U.S.

◄ In 1800, John Adams with his wife and family moved into the new official residence of the president. It later became known as the White House.

MRS. ADAMS

☆ Two members of Abigail Adams's family became U.S. presidents – her husband John, in 1796, and nearly thirty years later, their son John Quincy Adams.

Abigail Adams

merchant ships, it is not surprising that Adams and Jefferson had disagreements. Adams tried to keep the peace with Jefferson and worked to keep America out of foreign wars. He secretly sent three ambassadors to France in 1797 to draw up a treaty between the two countries. The French asked the ambassadors to bribe the French foreign minister with money to avoid war.

When Adams released this information to the public, war almost broke out between America and France. President Adams managed to reach an agreement with France to avoid total war, but he upset his own supporters. He had already upset Jefferson by signing the Alien and Sedition Acts, laws that did not allow criticism of the government.

IN RETIREMENT

By the end of his career, almost everyone in U.S. politics disliked Adams. In 1800, Thomas Jefferson defeated him in the presidential election. Adams then retired to Braintree, where he lived until his death. He died fifty years from the day the Declaration of Independence was signed.

THOMAS JEFFERSON

☆ **TERM**
1801–1809

☆ **PARTY**
Democratic-Republican

☆ **VICE PRESIDENTS**
*Aaron Burr,
George Clinton*

☆ **FIRST LADY**
None

☆ **STATES IN
THE UNION** *17*

> *The care of human life and happiness, and not their destruction, is the first and only legitimate object of good government.*

THOMAS JEFFERSON, 1809

THE FIDDLER
Jefferson was a keen musician who played the violin for up to three hours a day. He also liked gardening and grew many exotic crops on his estate.

Thomas Jefferson has as much claim to the title of "father of his country" as George Washington because he was the author of the Declaration of Independence and played a major role in setting up the new country. Yet Jefferson almost failed to become president at all. Born in 1743, he was a clever man who went to college and studied philosophy and law. Then he became a lawyer, and in 1769, he became a member of the Virginia legislature. Jefferson strongly believed that Americans had rights that their British rulers denied them. He published anti-British leaflets to tell the American people about his beliefs.

1743
Born in Albemarle County, Virginia

1762
Graduates from College of William and Mary

1769
Enters politics in Virginia

1775
Becomes a member of the Continental Congress

1776
Drafts Declaration of Independence

1779
Becomes governor of Virginia

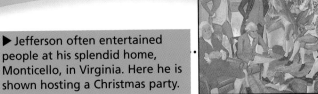
▶ Jefferson often entertained people at his splendid home, Monticello, in Virginia. Here he is shown hosting a Christmas party.

◀ In 1803, the United States bought the region called Louisiana from France. Lewis and Clark explored the area in their expedition of 1804–1806. The explorers' route can be seen on this map.

At first Jefferson was a great success. Taking little notice of the restrictions placed on his power, he made the **Louisiana Purchase** from the French, more than doubling the size of the United States. Anxious to know what this new land looked like, he sent explorers Lewis and Clark on a historic two-year expedition through this vast territory.

Jefferson was so popular that he was reelected president in 1804, but things soon went wrong. Britain and France were at war and were attacking U.S. shipping. To put pressure on the two countries, Jefferson banned all U.S. trade with them, but the U.S. economy suffered, and the ban was lifted before he left office in 1809.

In 1775, Jefferson became a member of the Continental Congress. Almost single-handedly, he wrote the Declaration of Independence, the foundation of the new republic. During the American **Revolutionary War**, he was governor of Virginia, and in 1785, he became his country's ambassador to France. There he saw the outbreak of the **French Revolution**, which he supported.

Back in America, Jefferson joined the government as **secretary of state** but quit because of his opposition to the pro-British attitude and strong government policies of Washington's Federalists. Jefferson was pro-French and was against a strong federal government. His beliefs led to the birth of the first U.S. opposition party – the Democratic-Republicans. This action started the **two-party political system** we see in government today.

EXPANDING THE COUNTRY

In 1796, Jefferson ran for president, but he was runner-up to his main rival, John Adams. As a result, he became vice president. In 1800, he ran for president again, but he won the same number of votes as another candidate, Aaron Burr. The House of Representatives considered the matter and narrowly elected Jefferson president.

TO MONTICELLO

On his retirement, Jefferson returned to Monticello, the beautiful house that he had designed and built himself. There he expanded his vast library, wrote numerous letters and books, and became a much-loved father figure until he died on July 4, 1826, the same day as his great rival, John Adams.

A GREAT DEMOCRAT

⭐ In 1776, Jefferson wrote the Declaration of Independence, one of the great documents in human history. It still influences people all around the world. He also wrote books, kept a huge library, and established the University of Virginia.

Writing the Declaration of Independence

789
Witnesses French Revolution as ambassador

1790–1793
Serves as secretary of state under Washington

1796
Elected vice president to John Adams

1800
Elected president

1803
Buys Louisiana Territory

1809
Retires as president

1826
Dies at Monticello, Virginia

LITTLE BIG MAN
James Madison weighed 100 lbs. (45 kg), and his friends said he was "no bigger than a half piece of soap." His wife called him her "darling little husband."

1751 Born in Port Conway, Virginia

1771 Graduates from New Jersey College, now Princeton

1780 Elected to Continental Congress

1787 Helps draft U.S. Constitution

1789 Elected to the House of Representatives from Virginia

1801 Becomes secretary of st under Preside Jefferson

Along with Washington, Adams, and Jefferson, James Madison played a vital role in establishing the newly independent United States of America. He was a clever scholar who read many books by European political thinkers. He put their ideas into practice in U.S. government.

Madison became a member of the Continental Congress in 1780. He developed the idea that governments needed to be kept under control. He believed that a system of checks and balances should control the three parts of government – leaders, lawmakers, and judges – to keep one part from getting too powerful. In this way, a strong leader could not ignore the law or the wishes of the people. These ideas were new at the time, but James Madison made sure that the U.S. Constitution, which was eventually signed in 1787, was based on this "separation of powers."

☆ **TERM** *1809–1817*

☆ **PARTY** *Democratic-Republican*

☆ **VICE PRESIDENTS** *George Clinton, Elbridge Gerry*

☆ **FIRST LADY** *Dolley Payne Todd*

☆ **STATES IN THE UNION** *19*

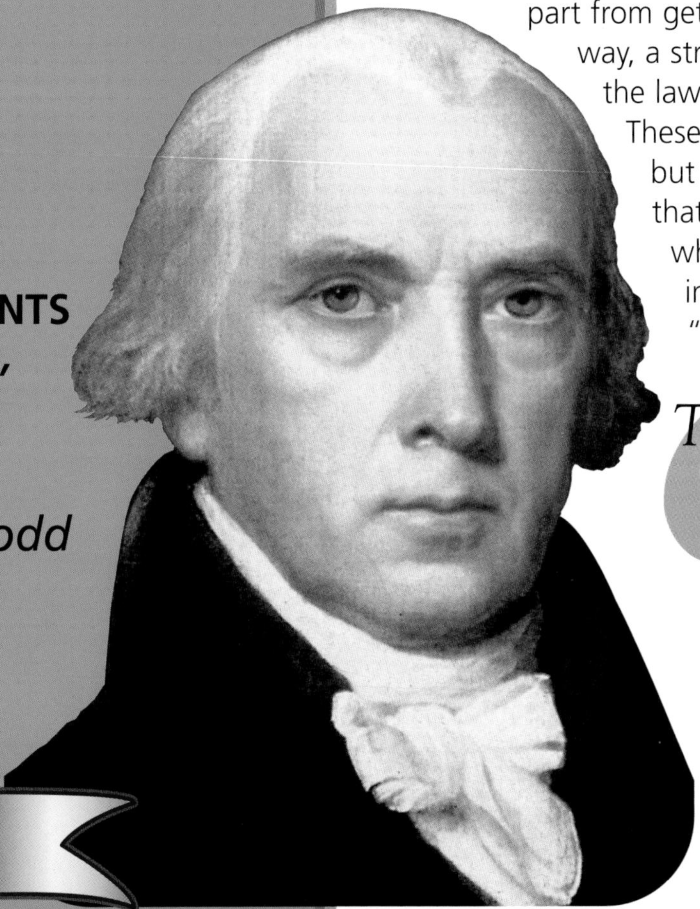

4th president

JAMES MADISON

"*The happy union of these states is a wonder; their Constitution a miracle; their example the hope of liberty throughout the world.*"

JAMES MADISON, 182

> ▶ During the burning of Washington in 1814, British troops blackened the president's residence. James Madison had the building painted white to hide the marks, so it became known as the White House.

808 ected esident	1812 Reelected president	1812–1814 Fights war against Britain	1817 Retires to Virginia	1836 Dies in Montpelier, Virginia

◀ The vessel USS *Constitution* (left) fights a British ship at the start of the War of 1812.

INTO OFFICE

In 1789, Madison was elected a member of the new House of Representatives. He was a close ally of Jefferson. When Madison left Congress in 1797, he fought hard against President Adams's Alien and Sedition Acts. Madison believed these laws stopped free speech. Thomas Jefferson became president in 1801 and made Madison his secretary of state. He served Jefferson loyally, and he was the natural successor when Jefferson stepped down. In 1808, Madison was elected as the fourth U.S. president.

Like Jefferson before him, Madison had to deal with the problem of the war between France and Great Britain and its effect on the United States. Although he tried not to take sides, this proved difficult to do, and in 1812, America declared war on Britain to stop it from attacking U.S. ships. The result was a disaster, as the small and badly led U.S. forces lost battle after battle. In 1814, the British attacked and burned parts of the U.S. capital, Washington, D.C., causing Madison's wife, Dolley, to flee the burning White House clutching a portrait of George Washington. The United States managed to win a major victory in the Battle of New Orleans, which raised morale considerably. Peace was eventually declared in 1815.

RETIREMENT

Madison spent the last two years of his presidency as a popular president, mainly because his country was becoming wealthier. He retired to Montpelier, Virginia, in 1817, living quietly there until his death in 1836.

THE STAR-SPANGLED BANNER

⭐ In September 1814, a young American lawyer, Francis Scott Key, boarded a British ship to bargain for the release of an American captured during the fighting between the two countries. While aboard, Key was forced to watch the British bombard a nearby fort. What he saw inspired him to write the words that in 1931 became the U.S. national anthem.

O, say can you see, by the dawn's early light,
What so proudly we hail'd at the twilight's last gleaming?
Whose broad stripes and bright stars through the perilous fight,
O'er the ramparts we watched were so gallantly streaming?
And the rockets' red glare, the bombs bursting in air,
Gave proof through the night that our flag was still there.
O, say does that star-spangled banner yet wave
O'er the land of the free and the home of the brave?

JAMES MONROE

☆ **TERM**
1817–1825

☆ **PARTY**
Democratic-Republican

☆ **VICE PRESIDENT**
Daniel Tompkins

☆ **FIRST LADY**
Elizabeth Kortright

☆ **STATES IN THE UNION** *24*

"...the American continents...are henceforth not to be considered as subjects for future colonization by any European powers."

JAMES MONROE, 1823

▲ The flag of 1818, when five new stars were added. There were 13 stripes, as there are today.

James Monroe was well equipped to become U.S. president. He had fought in the Revolutionary War and had been a senator, state congressman, governor (twice), secretary of state, war secretary, and ambassador. Above all, Monroe had been one of the two representatives who negotiated the purchase of the vast Louisiana Territory from France in 1803. As a lifelong friend of both presidents Jefferson and Madison, he was an ideal choice to follow Madison as president in 1817.

THE PEACEMAKER

Monroe was a great success as president. He was honest, friendly, tactful, and willing to work with both friends and opponents. He supported the pro-state, anti–big-government policies of Thomas Jefferson, which meant that he was happy for the individual states to govern themselves. But he also worked well with the Federalists. As a result, his first term as president became known as the "Era of Good Feelings."

As president, Monroe faced two major problems. The first was Florida, which was owned by Spain. Members of the **Seminole Nation,** who were living in Florida, regularly crossed the border and raided southern states. In 1818, U.S. troops

1758
Born in Westmoreland County, Virginia

1776–1780
Fights in U.S. Revolutionary War

1782
Enters politics in Virginia

1790
Elected to U.S. Senate

1794
Acts as ambassador to France

1799
Becomes governor of Virginia

1811
Appointed secretary of state under Madison

1816
Elected presiden

fought back, and war with Spain looked likely. In 1819, the Spanish agreed to hand over all of Florida east of the mighty Mississippi River to U.S. control. The second problem Monroe faced was **slavery**. Monroe disagreed with it, but he supported the **Missouri Compromise**, an agreement worked out in Congress. The compromise stated that the number of pro- and antislavery states in the **Union** must be the same. This agreement lasted until the 1850s.

INTO THE HISTORY BOOKS

One event that many people remember Monroe for is the **Monroe Doctrine**, which he set out in 1823. Many countries of Central and South America had gained their independence from Spain or Portugal, but America was concerned that strong European countries, such as Britain or France, might try to take over, or colonize, these new countries.

In December 1823, Monroe established a new U.S. foreign policy. He stated that the United States would not allow any European country to colonize the Americas or interfere with the governing of any of its countries. The Monroe Doctrine was regularly used in the following years to protect Latin America from being taken over by Europeans.

In 1825, Monroe stepped down as president. He was a much-loved man and was mourned by many people when he died in 1831. Like Presidents Adams and Jefferson before him, Monroe died on July 4, Independence Day.

THE MISSOURI COMPROMISE

★ Southern states such as Georgia allowed white people to keep African American people as slaves. These slaves were made to work for no pay and were not allowed human or civil rights. Northern states such as New York were against slavery. By 1820, the country was evenly split on this subject, as there were eleven slave states and eleven free states. In 1820, Congress agreed to let slaveowning Missouri and slave-free Maine join the Union, while slavery was still illegal in the northern part of the Louisiana Territory. A compromise was reached, and the balance between the equal numbers of pro- and antislavery states was maintained, but slavery continued to cause problems across the nation.

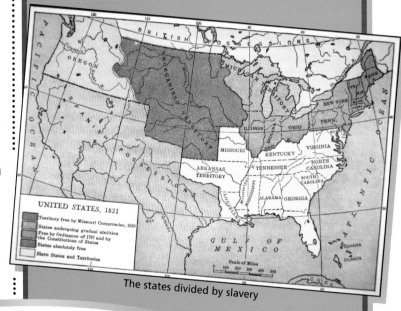

The states divided by slavery

Florida in the 1800s

1819
US acquires Florida from Spain

1820
Agrees to Missouri Compromise

1820
Reelected president

1823
Sets out Monroe Doctrine

1825
Retires from office

1831
Dies in New York City

► In 1823, an angel is said to have told Joseph Smith about a golden book. This event started the Mormon Church and Mormonism in America.

19

JOHN Q. ADAMS

6th president

⭐ **TERM**
1825–1829

⭐ **PARTY**
Democratic-Republican

⭐ **VICE PRESIDENT**
John Calhoun

⭐ **FIRST LADY**
Louisa Johnson

⭐ **STATES IN THE UNION** *24*

> *My whole life has been a succession of disappointments. I can scarcely recollect a single instance of success.*
>
> **JOHN QUINCY ADAMS, 1820**

John Quincy Adams was well qualified to become president. He was a gifted scholar, good at languages, and trained as a lawyer. Before becoming president, Adams was an ambassador to four European countries, and was a senator and secretary of state. He also negotiated the peace treaty with Britain that ended the War of 1812. In addition, his father, John Adams, was president before him and had trained John for the job. At age thirteen, Adams had even accompanied his father on diplomatic missions. But his own time as president was unsuccessful.

In the 1824 election, no candidate achieved a majority of votes. John Quincy Adams came second, as runner-up to Andrew Jackson. Early in 1825, the decision about who was to be president went

1767
Born in Braintree, Massachusetts

1787
Graduates from Harvard University

1790
Becomes a lawyer

1794
Ambassador to the Netherlands and later to Prussia, Russia, and Britain

1803
Elected to the Senate

1817
Becomes secretary of state under President Monroe

1824
Elected presiden

▶ In 1825, the Erie Canal was opened to traffic. The 363-mile canal linked Lake Erie and the other Great Lakes with New York and the East Coast.

to the House of Representatives, where each of the twenty-four states had one vote. The candidate in fourth place was Henry Clay, who made a deal with Adams. Clay said he would withdraw from the election if Adams made him secretary of state. Adams agreed and managed to beat Jackson and the remaining candidate by two votes.

ACCUSATIONS

Jackson was furious about the result and accused Henry Clay of betrayal. The argument raged for more than a year, and in 1826, Clay was forced to fight a duel with Senator John Randolph, who was a Jackson supporter. Randolph accused Clay of making a "corrupt bargain" with Adams. Neither was hurt in the duel. More important, Jackson continually accused Adams of corruption. This charge weakened Adams's government and eventually split his Democratic-Republican party in two – into the pro-Adams Whig Party and Jackson's Democrats.

BACK TO CONGRESS

As a result of his argument with Jackson, Adams did little in government and lost the election of 1828 to Jackson. In 1830, however, Adams won a seat in the House of Representatives. For eighteen

▲ In the election of 1824, Henry Clay withdrew after John Adams promised to make him secretary of state. Adams then went on to beat his rival, Andrew Jackson. This cartoon shows Henry Clay "silencing" Jackson by sewing up his mouth. It was meant to show how Clay did not give Jackson the chance to be president.

◄ The Last of the Mohicans, first published in 1826, was one of the most popular books in American literature. It tells the story of Hawkeye and his Mohican friends Uncas and Chingachgook.

years, he fought a campaign against the evils of slavery and won much respect for his tireless efforts.

In 1848, while making one of his many antislavery speeches in Congress, Adams collapsed and died, at age eighty.

LIKE FATHER, LIKE SON

☆ Like his father, John Adams, John Quincy Adams did not mean to be rude, but few people liked him. He was so unpopular that guests sometimes refused to come to his parties. His wife, Louisa, was a singer and harpist, but Adams described himself as "cold, austere, and forbidding." The couple are said to have argued about everything, especially the care of their children.

1828
loses presidential election

1830
Elected to the House of Representatives

1848
Dies in Washington, D.C.

1767
Born in
Waxhaw,
South
Carolina

1781
Fights in the
Revolutionary
War

1787
Becomes
a lawyer

1796
Represents
Tennessee in House
of Representatives

1815
Defeats the British at New Orleans
and becomes a major general

1823
Elected to
the Senate

1824
Loses presiden
election to Joh
Quincy Adam

▶ Jackson on horseback, fighting
at the Battle of New Orleans.

When Andrew Jackson was elected president in 1828, one of his former neighbors is said to have stated:

"If Andrew Jackson can become president, anyone can!" Jackson was rough and unruly as a young man, and he liked gambling and practical jokes. However, he was also a national hero. He fought in the Revolutionary War and defeated the British at the Battle of New Orleans in 1815.

Jackson's path to the White House was rough. He led in the election of 1824 but lost to John Quincy Adams. Jackson was successful in 1828, but his opponents turned the campaign into the first dirty election. They used details of Jackson's personal life to turn the public against him. They were able to do this because Jackson had married Rachel Robards twice – her divorce from her first husband was not finalized in time to make the first ceremony legal. Jackson's opponents accused his wife of bigamy, and she became ill as a result of the scandal. To Jackson's sadness, she died before he became president.

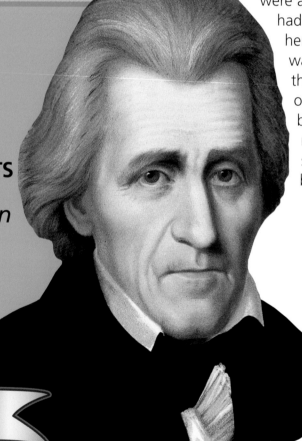

☆ **TERM**
1829–1837

☆ **PARTY**
Democratic

☆ **VICE PRESIDENTS**
*John Calhoun,
Martin Van Buren*

☆ **FIRST LADY**
None

☆ **STATES IN THE UNION** *26*

7th president

The great can protect themselves, but the poor and humble require the arm and shield of the law.

ANDREW JACKSON, 1821

ANDREW JACKSON

► Jackson's would-be assassin carried two pistols, both of which misfired, and Jackson shot him dead.

1828 Elected president

1832 Reelected president

1835 Survives assassination attempt

1837 Retires to his estate in Tennessee

1845 Dies in Nashville, Tennessee

BITING THE BULLET

For most of his adult life, Jackson lived with two bullets inside him. One was removed without anesthetic after twenty years; the other remained lodged near his heart until his death.

A MAN OF FIRSTS

☆ Andrew Jackson was the only U.S. president to kill a man in a duel (fought over his wife's honor), the only one to kill a man while in office (his would-be assassin), and the only one to be a prisoner of war (held by the British during the Revolutionary War).

INTO OFFICE

Jackson fought the 1828 election as head of the new **Democratic Party**, which workers, farmers, and small businesses supported. Jackson was in favor of the "little man" and against the political and business **establishment**. He won the election easily. At his **inauguration**, his supporters celebrated with such enthusiasm that the event almost turned into a riot.

As president, Jackson remained popular, but he was not a great success. He appointed a group of his friends to help him govern, and this team was known as a **kitchen cabinet**. These cabinet members rewarded their own friends by giving them well-paid government jobs, which led to accusations of **patronage** and corruption.

THE SURVIVOR

In 1835, an assassination attempt was made on Jackson – the first on a U.S. president – but he survived the attack and shot the assassin dead.

Jackson also showed that he was a political survivor when he refused to support Texas in its struggle for independence from Mexico. Texas allowed the people who lived in the region to keep slaves. Although he kept slaves himself and supported slavery, Jackson did not want to upset the balance between pro- and antislavery states in the Union by supporting Texas.

In 1837, Jackson retired to his estate. He was as popular at the end of his political life as he had been at the beginning.

FREE TEXAS

☆ In 1835, the Mexican province of Texas revolted and declared itself an independent republic. Within a year, Texas defeated the Mexican army and elected Sam Houston as its first president. The most famous battle in the Texas war of independence was in March 1836. The Mexican army besieged the Texans in the Alamo fortress. The Texans refused to surrender, and after a twelve-day bombardment, the Mexicans stormed the building and killed all 189 defenders.

The final few survivors make a last stand at the Alamo.

MARTIN VAN BUREN

☆ **TERM**
1837–1841

☆ **PARTY**
Democratic

☆ **VICE PRESIDENT**
Richard Johnson

☆ **FIRST LADY**
None

☆ **STATES IN THE UNION** *26*

1782
Born in Kinderhook, New York

1796
Leaves school with little formal education

1814
Elected to New York Senate

> *I cannot expect to perform the task with equal ability and success.*

MARTIN VAN BUREN ON TAKING OVER FROM ANDREW JACKSON IN 1837

THE FIRST AMERICAN

Martin Van Buren was the first U.S. president to be born an American citizen, as all his predecessors had been born British. He was also the only president who spoke Dutch as a first language.

Martin Van Buren was president for only four years. Many people believe that he did not achieve much of lasting value. Van Buren is best remembered as the man who set up a powerful organization called a **state machine**, which helped to get his candidates elected to office. He also helped establish the two-party U.S. political system that survives to this day.

Van Buren was born in New York state, the son of a farmer and innkeeper. He had little formal education and left school at age fourteen. Later, he learned enough law to become a lawyer. In 1814, he was elected to the New York **state senate** and progressed through the U.S. Senate. He became governor of New York state in 1828. Van Buren then set up a political organization known as the Albany Regency to tighten political control over New York.

Few people were allowed to vote in those days, so it was easy for Van Buren to make sure they voted in the way he wanted. Van Buren achieved control through a combination of discipline and patronage over voters. He used his organization to unite various groups and individuals who were opposed to John Quincy Adams as president, and he put together a winning election **campaign** for Andrew Jackson in 1828 and for himself in 1836.

When he set up the Democratic Party, Van Buren established the two-party system in American politics. The founding fathers who wrote the

1821
Elected to
U.S. Senate

1829
Becomes
governor of
New York

1829
Appointed secretary
of state under
Jackson

1832
Elected
vice president
under Jackson

1836
Elected
president

1840
Defeated by
William Harrison

1862
Dies in
Kinderhook,
New York

◀ Steamships began transatlantic service in 1838.

Constitution thought that individual members of Congress would have different ideas, so there was no need to have political parties. Martin Van Buren disagreed. He believed that two-party politics was the best way to make sure that issues were debated thoroughly and that both sides of an argument were fully discussed.

This style of politics and the combination of people that formed the basis for the Democratic Party is still used in U.S. politics today.

CAUTIOUS PROGRESS

As president, Van Buren was careful in everything he did. He inherited a financial crisis from Jackson, during which hundreds of banks went bankrupt. He solved the crisis by establishing firmer federal control over banks and gave the government more control over its own money. Although Van Buren was against slavery, he did nothing to anger the slaveowning states. He believed that slavery would end and that it would cause "terrible convulsions."

Van Buren preferred not to go to war with neighboring countries, so he worked hard to solve outstanding disputes with British-ruled Canada. In 1840, he ran for president again, but William Harrison defeated him.

FIXING THE RESULT

☆ Van Buren was very successful at "fixing things" in politics, meaning that he was good at getting people to vote the way he thought they should. He was known as "The Little Magician" and "The Fox of Kinderhook," which is where he was born and lived.

Many believe Van Buren lost this election because he refused to take over slaveowning Texas and because of a war being fought in Florida. He ran for president several times more but was never reelected. He died in Kinderhook in 1862.

▲ During Van Buren's presidency, about 18,000 members of the Cherokee Nation were removed from their eastern homelands to government-controlled Indian Territory west of the Mississippi River. About 4,000 of them died on this "Trail of Tears."

1773
Born in Charles
City County,
Virginia

1791
Joins the
army

1800
First governor
of Indiana
Territory

1811
Fights Native
Americans at
Tippecanoe
Creek

1812–1815
Fights British
and becomes a
brigadier general

1816
Elected to House
of Representatives
for Ohio

William Harrison holds three places in the record books. He is the second-oldest person ever to be elected president. (Only Ronald Reagan was older.) He also had the shortest term, and he was the first president to die in office. At his inauguration, Harrison caught a cold that turned into pneumonia and killed him thirty-two days later. Far more important than these records was the way that he ran his election campaign. The modern style of campaigning with slogans, posters, and handouts began with Harrison's campaign in 1840.

Harrison studied medicine, but at age eighteen he joined the army. For seven years, he fought the Native Americans of the Northwest Territory before resigning from the army in 1798. As a result of his efforts as a soldier, he was appointed first secretary of the Northwest Territory. When it was split into two, he became governor of Indiana, a post that he held for twelve years. During this time, he fought many battles with the Native Americans over land, including the battle at Tippecanoe Creek in 1811. This battle helped to give Harrison a national reputation, as did his role in defeating the British during the War of 1812.

☆ **TERM**
1841

☆ **PARTY**
Whig

☆ **VICE PRESIDENT**
John Tyler

☆ **FIRST LADY**
Anna Tuthill Symmes

☆ **STATES IN THE UNION** *26*

9th president

...with a supply of cider and a pension, he would happily sit by his log cabin for the rest of his days.

A POLITICAL OPPONENT, 1840

WILLIAM HARRISON

General Harrison defeats the allied force of British and Shawnee Indians at the Battle of the Thames River in 1813.

1825
Elected to Senate

1836
Loses presidential election to Van Buren

1840
Defeats Van Buren and is elected president

1841
Dies in Washington, D.C.

INTO POLITICS

Harrison used his military reputation to help his political career. In 1816, he was elected to the House of Representatives, and in 1825 he went to the Senate. After a brief time as ambassador to Colombia, he returned to politics as a leading member of the Whig Party. He fought and lost to Martin Van Buren in the 1836 presidential election but returned to fight again in 1840.

THE CAMPAIGNER

This time Harrison was determined to win. With a strong campaign slogan, he traveled around the country, meeting large numbers of voters. His rival, Van Buren, did the same, turning the election into the first two-party struggle for the presidency. It was also the first time that both candidates campaigned throughout the entire country.

While on the road, Harrison handed out campaign hats, mugs of hard cider, and model log cabins, and he taught his supporters a song called "Tippecanoe and Tyler, Too." It referred to his military victory of 1811 and to his running mate, John Tyler. One of its lines was "Van, Van is a used-up man,"

MORE FIRSTS

Along with other records, Harrison was the only president whose grandson also became president. His wife, Anna, was the first First Lady with any formal education.

because the Whigs thought their opponent was feeble and old compared with their rugged hero, Harrison. The election ended in a huge victory for Harrison, but his presidency was short-lived because he was not as rugged as he seemed. Harrison's death from pneumonia thirty-two days after his inauguration meant that he never had a chance to turn his ideas into action.

"LOG CABIN AND HARD CIDER"

☆ Harrison stumbled on his campaign slogan by accident. In 1840, he turned an opponent's criticism to his advantage by making "Log Cabin and Hard Cider" his campaign slogan. It appealed to people who enjoyed the simple pleasures in life. He ran his campaign from a log cabin on top of an open wagon. The voters were delighted that Harrison was handing out free mugs of hard cider (a popular alcoholic drink).

A book of 1841 named after Harrison's successful election slogan

John Tyler did not plan to become U.S. president. He gained the presidency when his running mate, William Harrison, died shortly after being elected. Tyler had been Harrison's running mate because Tyler was a southerner who helped Harrison to win much-needed votes from the southern, slaveowning states. As the first

▶ A former New York slave, Sojourner Truth, spoke out against slavery and for women's rights. Tyler thought each state should make its own laws on slavery.

president who was not actually elected, Tyler had little support from the public, and he was often criticized for his views. His nickname of "His Accidency" stayed with him throughout his term in office. Like many U.S. presidents, Tyler had trained as a lawyer and first entered politics through his **state assembly**. He rose through politics in Virginia to become governor and represented the state in both the House of Representatives and the Senate. Tyler was fiercely against federal control over the states and strongly supported their right to govern themselves. Tyler was not in favor of slavery, but he supported the right of the southern states to make their own laws on the subject. Tyler's views resulted in quarrels with Andrew Jackson and Martin Van Buren and led him to join the opposition party of William Harrison.

☆ **TERM**
1841–1845

☆ **PARTY**
Whig

☆ **VICE PRESIDENT**
None

☆ **FIRST LADIES**
Letitia Christian, Julia Gardiner

☆ **STATES IN THE UNION** *27*

10th president

JOHN TYLER

1840
Becomes vice president under Harrison

◄ The Lone Star was the flag of the former Texas republic. In 1844, Tyler asked Congress to approve the takeover of Texas, which occurred the following year.

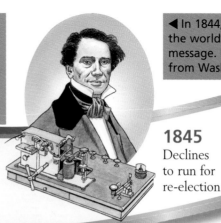

◄ In 1844, Samuel Morse sent the world's first telegraph message. It traveled forty miles, from Washington to Baltimore.

1841
Becomes president when Harrison dies

1845
Declines to run for re-election

1861
Chairs conference in Washington to avert a war

1862
Dies in Richmond, Virginia

THE UNEXPECTED PRESIDENT

The job of president was forced on Tyler at age fifty-one, and he was the youngest man until then to become president. But Tyler was not popular. He upset his Whig supporters by opposing the ideas that they supported, and he failed to gain support from the Democrats. However, he did enjoy some successes as president. He ended a war with the Seminole Nation in Florida, reorganized the U.S. Navy, reached a trade agreement with China, and encouraged settlers to move west across the Mississippi River to settle the vast prairies.

BABY BOOM

⭐ John Tyler had more children than any other president. His wife, Letitia Christian, had eight children before she died. Tyler then married Julia Gardiner, who was younger than three of Tyler's daughters, and they had seven more children.

Above all, Tyler began to take over the independent Republic of Texas. But Tyler had few political friends, and he decided not to fight the presidential election in 1844. Instead, he retired to his plantation in Virginia, but remained active in politics. In 1861, as the U.S. **Civil War** was about to break out, Tyler chaired a peace conference in Washington, D.C., between the pro- and antislavery states. The aim of the conference was to avoid a war between the northern and southern states over slavery, but it was not successful. When it failed, Tyler supported the southern states that decided to leave the Union. He was elected to the independent **Confederate** Congress in 1861, but he died before he could take his seat.

▲ In 1841, the first wagon train of sixty-nine pioneers crossed the Rocky Mountains on the Oregon Trail. By 1845, more than 5,000 people had journeyed to the west to settle in California and Oregon.

JAMES POLK

☆ **TERM**
1845–1849

☆ **PARTY**
Democratic

☆ **VICE PRESIDENT**
George Dallas

☆ **FIRST LADY**
Sarah Childress

☆ **STATES IN
THE UNION** *30*

1795
Born in
Mecklenburg
County, North
Carolina

1818
Graduates from
university and
practices law

1823
Enters politic
in Tennessee

> *...though I occupy
> a very high position,
> I am the hardest-
> working man in
> the country*

JAMES POLK, 1845

In 1841, James Polk's
**political career looked like it was
over. He was defeated in his fight to be**
reelected governor of Tennessee after two years
in office, and even worse, he was defeated again
when he tried to regain the governorship in 1843.
Yet, at the 1844 Democratic Party Convention, Polk
was nominated to run for president and went on to
win the election narrowly. Polk owed
his win at the convention to his
opponent's views on Texas.
Martin Van Buren was opposed
to bringing Texas into the Union
because it was a proslavery
state. This would upset the
balance between pro- and
antislavery states in the Union.
Polk wanted to annex Texas, or add

**TRUST
NO BANK**
James Polk did not trust
banks; he kept all his
money in bags around the
house. When he died, he
left all the money he
had to his wife,
Sarah.

it to the Union, and was finally
nominated as a candidate on the
ninth **ballot**. As candidate, Polk campaigned on a
slogan of "54–40 or fight," which referred to the
latitude of the boundary line between British-run
Canada and the northwestern territory of Oregon.
Both Britain and the United States claimed Oregon,
and as a result, war between the two looked
possible. Polk won the election and was determined
to expand the Union as much as he could. In 1845,
a journalist named John O'Sullivan wrote an article
in which he said that it was "our manifest destiny
to overspread the continent allotted by Providence
for the free development of our yearly multiplying
millions." Polk agreed with O'Sullivan and took
charge of the biggest U.S. expansion since Jefferson
bought the Louisiana Territory in 1803.

Texas eventually joined the Union in 1845 as the
twenty-eighth state, but Polk wanted to own the

1825
Elected to
House of
Representatives

1835
Becomes
Speaker of
the House

1839
Elected
governor of
Tennessee

1841, 1843
Fails to win
reelection as
governor

1844
Elected
president

1849
Steps down as
president and
soon dies

▶ From 1845 to 1849, Ireland suffered a terrible famine, and up to one million Irish people moved to America.

THE WORKAHOLIC

☆ James Polk worked hard. His wife, Sarah, also worked hard as his private secretary and chief adviser. Polk refused to run for a second presidential term and died, exhausted after all his efforts, about three months after leaving office.

☆ James Polk was the first president to have "Hail to the Chief" played when he arrived at official occasions. He also hosted the first Thanksgiving dinner at the White House. He banned alcohol, music, and dancing at his parties, and he was said to have had no sense of humor.

Mexican provinces to its west, notably California. He offered Mexico $30 million for the region, but Mexico rejected the offer. Polk then sent General Zachary Taylor to stir things up, and war between the two countries broke out in 1846. The fight was short and one-sided. By early 1848, the two countries signed the Treaty of Guadalupe Hidalgo, under which Mexico was forced to hand over 500,000 square miles of territory in return for $15 million. The area included the whole of what is now California, Nevada, and Utah plus much of New Mexico, Arizona, Wyoming, and Colorado.

Meanwhile, Polk had peacefully settled the Oregon dispute with Britain by agreeing to set the border along the more southerly forty-ninth latitude. The United States now reached from the Atlantic to the Pacific and governed everything between Canada and Mexico.

James Polk always said he would be president for only one term. He said at his inauguration that "though I occupy a very high position, I am the hardest-working man in the country." By 1849, he was exhausted. He retired to his estate in Nashville, Tennessee, and died a few months later.

◀ At the battle of Resaca de la Palma, in Texas, the U.S. Army fought the Mexican army for four days before the official declaration of war on May 13, 1846.

ZACHARY TAYLOR

12th president

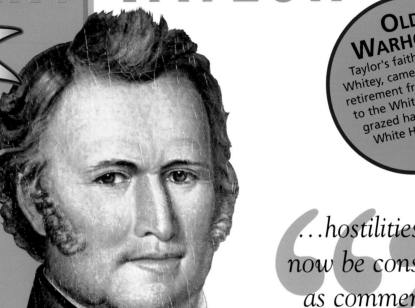

★ **TERM**
1849–1850

★ **PARTY**
Whig

★ **VICE PRESIDENT**
Millard Fillmore

★ **FIRST LADY**
Margaret Smith

★ **STATES IN
THE UNION** *30*

OLD WARHORSE
Taylor's faithful horse, Whitey, came with him in retirement from the army to the White House and grazed happily on the White House lawn.

...hostilities may now be considered as commenced.

ZACHARY TAYLOR, 1846

Like Andrew Jackson and William Harrison before him, Zachary Taylor **became president because of his military** reputation. Since Taylor's presidency was so short, he is best remembered for his military achievements.

A NATIONAL HERO
Zachary Taylor was raised in Kentucky and joined the army in 1808, at age twenty-four. He remained in the army for forty years, fighting the British in the War of 1812 and Native Americans in many conflicts around the Union.

By the mid-1840s, he was a much-admired military leader and was known as "Old Rough and Ready" for his down-to-earth approach. The war against Mexico solidified his reputation as a great leader. In 1846, he advanced into Mexico on President Polk's orders. The plan was to force Mexico to declare war on the United States. He achieved this aim and telegraphed Polk, "[H]ostilities may now be considered as commenced." This told Polk that war had started.

Taylor defeated the Mexicans at Palo Alto and Resaca de la Palma, then took their stronghold of Monterrey. In 1847, he achieved his greatest victory when he defeated a force that was four times greater than his own at Buena Vista. By the time the war ended in 1848, Taylor was a national hero.

1784
Born in Orange County, Virginia

1808
Joins the U.S. army

1810
Becomes a captain

1812
Promoted to major for his defense of Fort Harrison

1832
Becomes a colonel

1846–1848
Commands army war against Mex

THE GOLD RUSH

⭐ In March 1848, the first newspaper reports appeared about the discovery of gold near the American River in California. Within a year, about 80,000 people headed to California to seek their fortune. About 10,000 Australians crossed the Pacific Ocean, while many more prospectors arrived from Europe, Asia, and South America. Some became rich, but many lost their money on gambling and other illegal activities.

Early gold prospectors try their luck.

A GOOD CAMPAIGN

The Whig Party was keen to regain the presidency in 1848 from the Democrats, who had captured it from them four years earlier. To achieve this goal, they convinced Taylor to stand for them in the presidential election. Taylor had never even voted in a presidential election, but he ran a good campaign and won the election.

As president, Taylor governed a country that was increasingly divided on the problem of slavery. He was a southerner and kept slaves himself, so he was happy for existing slaveowning states to keep slavery. But Taylor believed that slavery should not be allowed in any new states that wanted to join the Union.

In July 1850, before he had time to settle this sensitive issue, Taylor died. He was sixty-five. Taylor had achieved little of lasting importance during his one-and-a-half years as president.

◀ Zachary Taylor, dressed in uniform as an American army commander on his horse, Whitey. Taylor was well known across the Union for his heroics in battle, in particular during the Mexican War of 1846–1848.

1848
Elected president

1850
Dies in Washington, D.C.

▲ In 1849, during Taylor's presidency, twenty people died in riots outside the Astor Place Opera House in New York City.

MILLARD FILLMORE

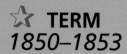

13th president

⭐ **TERM**
1850–1853

⭐ **PARTY**
Whig

⭐ **VICE PRESIDENT**
None

⭐ **FIRST LADY**
Abigail Powers

⭐ **STATES IN THE UNION** *31*

A WORKING LADY

Millard Fillmore's wife, Abigail, was the first First Lady to have a job. She worked as a teacher. She met her future husband when he returned to school at age nineteen to finish his education.

Millard Fillmore **became president when Zachary Taylor died. Fillmore's own term in** office was short, and it was totally dominated by the subject of slavery. He was not a strong enough president to bring a solution to this problem.

EARLY LIFE

Fillmore was born and brought up in New York. He was not well educated, although he trained as a lawyer while in his early twenties. As a member of the New York state assembly, he made himself popular by sponsoring a government bill that changed the law so that people who were in debt could not be imprisoned. In 1833, Fillmore was elected to the House of Representatives, where he joined the Whigs and was a useful party member. He was a natural choice to become the vice presidential candidate under Zachary Taylor, but he was ill prepared to become president himself.

▶ In 1851, a U.S. yacht, the *America*, beat fourteen British yachts in a race around the Isle of Wight, England. The race is now called the America's Cup.

Timeline

1800
Born in Cayuga County, New York

1823
Becomes a lawyer

1829
Elected to New York state assembly

1833
First elected to House of Representatives

1848
Elected vice president under Zachary Taylor

1850
Becomes president on Taylor's death

THE COMPROMISER

As president, Fillmore had to face the problem of slavery, which was rapidly tearing the Union apart. Fillmore wanted to reach an agreement between the two sides and was willing to compromise to get it. Congress debated the subject for months before Fillmore eventually agreed to a series of proposals, known as the Compromise of 1850.

The compromise allowed California to join the Union as a free state, let New Mexico and Utah make their own choices, and abolished slavery in the District of Columbia. The compromise also included the Fugitive Slave Act, which required people to return runaway slaves to their original owners from anywhere in the country. Fillmore enforced this act firmly, upsetting antislavery campaigners in the northern states. The compromise did, however, make the southern states more content.

▶ President Fillmore's wife, Abigail Powers, was responsible for setting up a library in the White House.

CLASSIC LITERATURE

☆ *Moby-Dick, or, The Whale* was published by Herman Melville in 1851. It tells the tale of Captain Ahab and his pursuit of a white whale. Although difficult to read and slow to sell, the book soon became a classic of American literature.

In 1852, readers flocked to buy *Uncle Tom's Cabin, or, Life among the Lowly*. The story, by Harriet Beecher Stowe, was about an African American slave who rescues a white child. The book sold 300,000 copies the first year it was published and was made into a play.

Sales advertisement for Stowe's classic story

135,000 SETS, 270,000 VOLUMES SOLD.

UNCLE TOM'S CABIN

FOR SALE HERE.

AN EDITION FOR THE MILLION, COMPLETE IN 1 Vol, PRICE 37 1-2 CENTS.
" " IN GERMAN, IN 1 Vol, PRICE 50 CENTS.
" " IN 2 Vols, CLOTH, 6 PLATES, PRICE $1.50.
SUPERB ILLUSTRATED EDITION, IN 1 Vol, WITH 153 ENGRAVINGS,
PRICES FROM $2.50 TO $5.00.

The Greatest Book of the Age.

TO JAPAN

In 1852, Fillmore sent Commodore Matthew Perry to Japan to force the Japanese to open up their ports to western shipping and trade. A treaty between the two countries was signed in 1854, opening up trade links and ending about 150 years of Japanese isolation.

IN RETIREMENT

Fillmore had hoped to make the Whigs an obvious choice to run the government, as it was a compromise party between the proslavery and antislavery forces. His party failed to renominate him for the presidency in 1852, however, and he stepped down as president.

He fought for the presidency again as an Independent in 1856 but got little support and retired to Buffalo, New York, where he was active in local affairs until his death.

350
rees to
very
npromise

1852
Fails to be renominated for president by his Whig Party

1856
Runs for president again

1874
Dies in Buffalo, New York

1804
Born in Hillsboro, New Hampshire

1827
Becomes a lawyer

1829
Enters politics in New Hampshire

1833
Elected to House of Representatives

1837
Elected to Senate

▶ In 1853, Commodore Perry met representatives of the Japanese emperor in Japan. A treaty between the two countries was signed in 1854.

In 1852, half the states in the Union were against slavery and the other half were for slavery. As this subject continued to divide the northern and southern states, the United States needed a strong president. Instead, the people elected Franklin Pierce, a compromise candidate – a man who won his party's nomination only on the forty-ninth ballot.

☆ **TERM**
1853–1857

☆ **PARTY**
Democratic

☆ **VICE PRESIDENT**
William King

☆ **FIRST LADY**
Jane Appleton

☆ **STATES IN THE UNION** *31*

14th president

THE COMPROMISE
Franklin Pierce made his reputation as a politician in New Hampshire. He was also an effective member of both the House of Representatives and the Senate. In addition, he fought in the Mexican War. Although he represented a northern state – New Hampshire – he actually supported the slaveowners of the South. In theory, that made him an ideal candidate to unite both his own party and the country, and he won the presidential election in 1852 by a **landslide** against his Whig opponent.

KANSAS AND NEBRASKA
Once in office, Pierce supported the slaveowners but failed to stop the rising opposition to slavery. He also failed to unite his country. In 1854, he approved the Kansas–Nebraska Act, which overturned the Missouri Compromise of 1820. The act allowed the territories in the northern part of the old Louisiana Purchase to choose whether to allow slavery. Until then, they had not been allowed to

HOME COMFORTS
Pierce and his wife did much to modernize the White House, installing central heating and a second bathroom. Pierce was also the first president to have a Christmas tree in the White House.

FRANKLIN PIERCE

▶ In the poem *The Song of Hiawatha*, published in 1855, Henry Wadsworth Longfellow told of a Native American hero and his love, Minnehaha.

▶ In 1853, Levi Strauss began to sell heavyweight cotton trousers to miners in California. These were the first blue jeans.

1846–1848
Fights in Mexican War

1852
Wins presidential election

1854
Approves Kansas–Nebraska Act

1856
Not renominated as Democratic candidate

1869
Dies in Concord, New Hampshire

make this decision. A local war almost started in Kansas, and riots broke out in Boston and in other cities that were against the act. Many people threatened to disobey the Fugitive Slave Act and not return runaway slaves to their owners.

ONE SUCCESS

In 1853, Pierce had a great success when he negotiated the **Gadsden Purchase** from Mexico for $10 million. Through this purchase, the United States gained about 30,000 square miles of territory west of Texas. The land allowed the important southern railroad to California to pass entirely through U.S. territory.

Pierce planned to take over Cuba (owned by Spain) if a slave revolt there spread to the southern United States. This upset many people, and other mistakes almost caused a war with both Spain and Great Britain. As a result, Pierce's own party did not renominate him for president, and he retired. He died in 1869.

THE REPUBLICAN PARTY

☆ In 1854, a group of Democrats and Whigs who were against slavery met in Ripon, Wisconsin. They agreed that if the Kansas–Nebraska Act became law, they would form a new party to fight against slavery. The act did become law, and the new party was formed. It was called the Republican Party. The party held its first state convention in Jackson, Michigan, in July 1854 and ran its first presidential campaign in 1856. The group chose the name "Republican" in honor of Thomas Jefferson, the first Democratic–Republican president, who was an opponent of slavery, even though he kept slaves himself.

▶ Throughout the southern states, African Americans were forced to work as slaves on cotton and fruit plantations.

JAMES BUCHANAN

15th president

1791
Born near
Mercersburg,
Pennsylvania

1821
Elected to House
of Representatives

1832
Becomes
ambassador
to Russia

1834
Elected
to Senate

☆ **TERM**
1857–1861

☆ **PARTY**
Democratic

☆ **VICE PRESIDENT**
John Breckinridge

☆ **FIRST LADY**
None

☆ **STATES IN
THE UNION** *33*

> *If you are as happy on entering this house as I am at leaving it…you are the happiest man in this country.*

**JAMES BUCHANAN TO
ABRAHAM LINCOLN, 1861**

When he was elected president in 1856, James Buchanan was probably the wrong person to lead his country. He was a proslavery Democrat who favored the southern states, but his policies failed to keep his country together.

Buchanan had trained as a lawyer and made his reputation in the House of Representatives and the Senate. He also served as ambassador to Russia and then to Great Britain.

While Buchanan was in Britain in 1854, a slave revolt in Spanish-owned Cuba threatened to spread to the southern states of America. Buchanan met secretly with the U.S. ambassadors to France and Spain. They decided to push Spain to sell Cuba to the United States. If Spain refused to sell the island, America would take it by force. Cuba would then become a slaveowning state in the Union.

The ambassadors' secret plan, called the Ostend Manifesto, soon became public. This manifesto angered Americans who were opposed to slavery, and the government rejected it. Still, Buchanan's plan gained him great popularity in the southern states. As a result, he won the Democratic nomination for presidency.

A NATION DIVIDED

As president, Buchanan governed a country that was split between pro- and antislavery states. Buchanan believed that the federal government had no right to tell the slave states what laws they should live by. He thought that territories joining the Union should decide for themselves whether to allow slavery.

1845
Secretary of state under Polk

1853
Ambassador to Great Britain

1856
Wins presidential election for Democrats

1859
John Brown is hanged in Virginia

1861
Steps down as president

1868
Dies in Lancaster, Pennsylvania

► The world's first oil well was drilled in Pennsylvania by Edwin Drake (in top hat) in 1859.

▲ In 1860 the first Pony Express carried mail from Missouri to California.

In 1857, in a case known as the Dred Scott case, the U.S. **Supreme Court** ruled that slaves and their descendants were property, not people. In addition, the court ruled that the Missouri Compromise of 1820 was unconstitutional, or against the rules in the Constitution. This was because the Constitution gave rights to all states to keep slaves, whereas the compromise did not allow slavery in the northern part of the Louisiana Purchase.

Buchanan made things worse by approving a proslavery constitution for Kansas. He also harshly enforced the Fugitive Slave Act. By 1859, the country was in turmoil.

JOHN BROWN'S UPRISING

In October 1859, John Brown and a group of militant **abolitionists** seized an arsenal, or a supply of weapons, at Harper's Ferry in Virginia. They planned to use the weapons to help slaves win their freedom by fighting against their owners. John Brown was captured and hanged in December 1859. His actions caused fears in the South that abolitionists in the North wanted to bring about an uprising by the slaves in their states.

▲ On December 2, 1859, the antislavery campaigner John Brown (kissing child) was led from his prison cell in Charleston, West Virginia, taken to the gallows, and hanged.

THE SINGLE PRESIDENT

★ James Buchanan never married, so his niece, Harriet Lane, was hostess at his White House parties. People thought Buchanan might be lonely in the White House, so they sent him pets for company, including a pair of bald eagles and a Newfoundland dog.

A DIVIDED COUNTRY

In 1860, the two parties chose their candidates for the forthcoming presidential election. The new **Republican Party** chose Abraham Lincoln, who was against slavery. The Democrats were divided, and they chose two opposing candidates – the proslavery, current vice president, John Breckinridge, and Senator Stephen Douglas, who believed that states should choose for themselves whether to keep slaves.

Lincoln won, and the country finally split into two. The Civil War was about to begin.

1809
Born in
Hardin County,
Kentucky

1830
Moves to
Illinois

1834–1842
Member of the
Illinois state
legislature

1847
Enters U.S.
House of
Representatives

1856
Joins
Republican
Party

1858
Challenges
Stephen
Douglas to
debates

1860
Elected
president

◀ The log cabin where President
Lincoln was born in 1809

At the most difficult time in its history,
the United States of America elected
as president a man who came from a
poor family, had little formal schooling, and had
only two years' experience in national politics.
Yet Abraham Lincoln did the job well, and many
people believe that he is the finest president
the United States has ever had.

FROM A LOG CABIN TO THE LAW

Lincoln was born in a log cabin in Kentucky. His
family moved to Indiana, where Lincoln educated
himself, reading the Bible, Shakespeare, and many
other books. In 1830, he moved to Illinois and
trained as a lawyer, setting up a legal practice in
1837. He was elected to the state legislature, but
he did not make much of the job. After eight
years, he returned to work in the law.

ANTISLAVERY POLITICS

In 1847, Lincoln entered the U.S.
House of Representatives. He was
not a great success and returned to
Illinois in 1849. He entered national
politics for the second time in 1854,
when Illinois senator Stephen Douglas
put the Kansas–Nebraska Act through
Congress. This law legalized slavery.
Lincoln was against slavery and did not

☆ **TERM**
1861–1865

☆ **PARTY**
Republican

☆ **VICE PRESIDENTS**
*Hannibal Hamlin,
Andrew Johnson*

☆ **FIRST LADY**
Mary Todd

☆ **STATES IN
THE UNION** *36*

16th president

*…this nation, under
God, shall have
a new birth
of freedom…*

**FROM LINCOLN'S
GETTYSBURG ADDRESS,
NOVEMBER 19, 1863**

ABRAHAM LINCOLN

▶ Lincoln's famous address in Gettysburg in 1863 lasted only a few minutes.

▶ Lincoln (center) was shot in a Washington theater by John Wilkes Booth (left).

1865
Killed in Ford's Theater, Washington, D.C.

1861
Civil War breaks out

1863
Emancipation Proclamation to free slaves takes effect

1863
Delivers Gettysburg Address

1864
Reelected president

want it to spread to the western territories. He joined the new, antislavery Republican Party, and in a series of debates, he challenged Douglas for his Senate seat. "I believe this government cannot endure permanently half slave and half free," he said. Lincoln won the debates, but he lost the election. By now, he was a national figure, and in 1860, he was chosen as the Republican candidate for president. When he won, eleven southern states left the Union, and the Civil War broke out.

FREEING THE SLAVES

Lincoln wanted to keep the Union together, and at first, he did nothing about slavery. His government was split between abolitionists and supporters of the Confederates.

THE CIVIL WAR

⭐ When Abraham Lincoln became president in 1861, South Carolina and ten other proslavery southern states left the Union and formed the Confederacy. On April 12, Confederate forces attacked the Union forces at Fort Sumter, South Carolina. War broke out. The Confederates were led by Robert E. Lee and Thomas "Stonewall" Jackson. At first they won most of the battles, but by 1864 the Union forces under General Ulysses Grant took control and won the four-year war in 1865.

Union flag used at Fort Sumter   Flag of the Confederacy

DEATH THREATS

⭐ As president, Lincoln received more than 10,000 death threats. He kept some of them in his desk at the White House, in an envelope marked "Assassinations." In response to these threats, he said: "I cannot bring myself to believe that any human being lives who would do me any harm."

Lincoln did not take either side at first, but after several victories, he signed the Emancipation Proclamation, which set all slaves free. In reality, the proclamation meant nothing. Lincoln had no constitutional authority to abolish slavery, and he did not have any power over the **Confederacy**. But the proclamation turned the war from a fight over **secession** to a fight over the legality of slavery.

VICTORY AND DEATH

Lincoln did not want a war. With his Gettysburg Address, he dedicated a cemetery to those who had died in battle. His speech proclaimed "a new birth of freedom" in America. Lincoln did not live to see that freedom. A week after the Confederate army surrendered in 1865, southerner John Wilkes Booth assassinated Lincoln in Washington, D.C.

▶ The Fifty-Fourth Massachusetts, the first African American regiment after emancipation, stormed Fort Wagner in 1863.

ANDREW JOHNSON

* **TERM**
1865–1869

* **PARTY**
Democratic

* **VICE PRESIDENT**
None

* **FIRST LADY**
Eliza McCardle

* **STATES IN THE UNION** *37*

His faith in people never wavered.

EPITAPH ON HIS GRAVESTONE

SEWN UP
Throughout his life, Andrew Johnson made his own suits and was skilled at needlework and making quilts.

The Civil War made, and also destroyed, Andrew Johnson. He was the only southern state senator to remain loyal to the Union, and he became a hero to those who were struggling to keep the country united during the Civil War. Yet after the war, Johnson failed to lead the country to a peaceful future.

TAILORED FOR OFFICE
Andrew Johnson was born into a poor family, and at age fourteen, he was apprenticed to a tailor. He soon set up his own tailor's shop. When he was nineteen, he married sixteen-year-old Eliza McCardle. Eliza set out to educate her husband, even teaching him to write. In 1828, Johnson became alderman of Greenville, Tennessee, and then mayor, starting a public career in the Democratic Party that lasted for more than forty years. Unlike most southerners, he was opposed to the slaveowners and did not wish to extend slavery to the new territories in the West.

HIS FINEST HOUR
Johnson's finest hour came in 1861. As senator for Tennessee, he was expected to join the Confederacy when the Civil War broke out. But Johnson was a strong supporter of the Union and remained in the U.S. Senate. As a reward, Johnson was appointed military governor of Tennessee. Before the end of the war, he was able to set up a new local government in Tennessee to take over for the U.S. Army.

1808
Born in Raleigh, North Carolina

1835
Enters politics in Tennessee

1843
Elected to House of Representatives

1853
Governor of Tennessee

1857
Elected to Senate

1861
Remains in Senate after Tennessee joins Confederacy

1864
Elected vice president to Lincoln

1865
Becomes president Lincoln's death

FIRST IMPEACHMENT

⭐ In 1868, Andrew Johnson was the first and until Bill Clinton, the only president to face impeachment by Congress, which means they tried to remove him from office. He was charged with "high crimes and misdemeanors." The Senate was one vote short of the number it needed to convict him, so Johnson remained in office.

Ticket to Johnson's impeachment

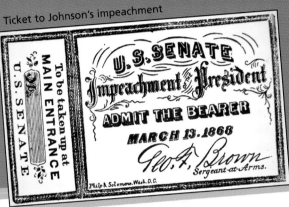

In 1864, Abraham Lincoln made Johnson his running mate in the presidential election. This provided a balance between a northern Republican president and a southern Democratic vice president.

On the assassination of President Lincoln, Johnson became president. He faced an impossible task of fixing the many problems left by the war.

Politically, Johnson had few friends. Southerners and Democrats thought he was a traitor, and Northerners and Republicans distrusted him for his southern ideals. Both sides thought he was too rigid in his views and not clever enough to run the country at such a time. Only a man like Lincoln could have coped with all the problems – and Johnson was not such a strong president.

A CLASH OF VIEWS

As president, Johnson faced an angry Congress. It overruled him on many occasions and passed the Tenure of Office Act to keep him from dismissing officials that Congress had approved. In 1867, events came to a head when the secretary of war, Edwin Stanton, told him that the military governors in charge of the southern states were answerable to Congress and not to the president. Johnson fired Stanton, breaking the Tenure of Office Act. This led to Johnson's **impeachment** before Congress. He just managed to keep his job.

NORTHERN SUCCESS

The main success of Johnson's term of office came in 1867, when he bought the vast northern territory of Alaska from Russia for $7 million. But this was a minor triumph, and Johnson did not seek reelection as president. Instead, he retired to Tennessee. Johnson returned to the Senate in 1875, but he died soon after taking his Senate post.

RECONSTRUCTION

⭐ After the Civil War ended, Johnson and Congress began to rebuild and reform the southern states in a program known as Reconstruction. This slowly restored civilian government to the states and allowed them to rejoin the Union. In 1868, the Fourteenth Amendment to the Constitution became law. It granted full citizenship to former slaves. However, many southern states continued to deny African American people the right to vote or serve in state governments.

1868
Senate fails to remove him after impeachment

1869
Steps down as president

◀ Cartoonists joked that Johnson would have to ask polar bears to vote for him in the empty state of Alaska.

◀ In 1868, the Sioux signed a peace treaty.

1875
Returns to the Senate

1875
Dies in Carter's Station, Tennessee

ULYSSES GRANT

⭐ **TERM**
1869–1877

⭐ **PARTY**
Republican

⭐ **VICE PRESIDENTS**
*Schuyler Colfax,
Henry Wilson*

⭐ **FIRST LADY**
Julia Dent

⭐ **STATES IN
THE UNION** *38*

Let us have peace.

**PRESIDENTIAL ACCEPTANCE
SPEECH, 1868**

NEW NAME GRANT

Grant was originally named Hiram Ulysses Grant, but at West Point, he discovered that he had been registered as Ulysses Simpson Grant. He kept his new name for the rest of his life.

Ulysses Grant was
**the man who won the Civil War for
the Union. He was rewarded by being**
elected president twice. Although he remained
popular throughout his eight years, Grant had his
problems as president. In fact, his government was
often rocked by scandal.

CONSTANT FAILURE

Grant was the son of a leather tanner. He was
not especially talented as a child and
when he graduated from the
famous West Point

military academy, his only
real skill was horse riding.
In 1843, Grant entered
the army and fought in
the Mexican War of 1846 to 1848. He eventually
resigned in disgrace in 1854. After the war, he was
posted to the West Coast and began drinking too
much. Grant then went to work for his father, and
his military career seemed to be over.

In 1861, Grant rejoined the army to fight for the
Union in the Civil War. He discovered that he had a
natural ability to lead a large army in a difficult war.

▶ In 1870, Wyoming gave
women the right to vote. Louisa
Swain became the first American
woman to vote in an election.

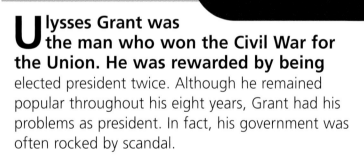

1822
Born in Point
Pleasant, Ohio

1843
Graduates from the
U.S. Military Academy,
West Point, New York

1854
Forced to resign
from the army for
excessive drinking

1861
Rejoins army
at start of
Civil War

1864
Takes
command of
Union forces

1868
Wins
presidency for
Republicans

In the western territories, settlers and Native Americans were struggling bitterly over who owned the land. The growth of industry in the big cities was changing the economy in the North dramatically, and this also caused many problems.

Grant was not experienced in politics, and he did not cope well with these challenges. He appointed to the cabinet his friends and supporters, who soon took bribes. Although Grant was an honest man, the members of his government were not, and they were attacked from all sides.

▲ On May 10, 1869, the Union Pacific and Central Pacific railroads met at Promontory, Utah. The railroad linked the East Coast and West Coast for the first time. A golden spike was hammered into the final railroad tie to celebrate the historic occasion.

He captured the Confederate Fort Donelson in 1862, telling its commander, "No terms except an unconditional and immediate surrender can be accepted." He earned the nickname "Unconditional Surrender" Grant, and by 1864, he was in charge of all the Union forces. On April 9, 1865, the Confederate forces led by General Robert E. Lee surrendered to Grant at Appomattox Court House, Virginia.

IN RETIREMENT

In 1876, the Republicans chose another candidate for president, and Grant retired. He went on a successful world tour, but on his return he invested money in a corrupt bank that went out of business. Grant was bankrupt and dying of cancer, so he hurriedly wrote a book about his life to provide for his wife and family. The book was published a few days before his death, becoming a huge success. This proved that despite his mistakes as president, Grant was a much-loved figure whose military career had saved the Union from collapse.

PRESIDENTIAL SCANDAL

Grant was a hero of the Union. The Republicans chose him for the 1868 election, which he won easily. The country needed a strong, firm leader because it was going through many changes.

In the South, **Reconstruction** made life even more difficult than before for African Americans.

SILENTLY SQUEAMISH

⭐ Although he spent much of his life in the army and in battle, Grant hated the sight of blood and as a child refused to work in his father's tannery.

⭐ As president, Grant was a man of few words. For one speech, he just said, "Gentlemen, in response it will be impossible to do more than thank you," and sat down.

1872
Reelected president

1877
Steps down as president

1877–1879
Tours the world

1880
Fails to gain nomination for presidency

1885
Dies at Mount McGregor, New York

◀ General George Custer and about 250 U.S. soldiers were killed at Little Big Horn, in Montana, by 2,500 Sioux and Cheyenne Indians in June 1876.

45

Rutherford Hayes became a national figure as governor of Ohio, where he proved that he was an able and competent administrator and reformer. He was honest but dull, yet the way he ran the country was controversial from the first day.

THE END OF RECONSTRUCTION

The circumstances of Hayes's election were most unusual. The vote was close, and in the end it appeared that Hayes was runner-up in both popular and electoral votes. Yet, in the end, a special commission declared Hayes the winner by one electoral vote. (See box on page 47.)

The opposition Democrats were outraged, calling Hayes "His Fraudulency" and his election "The Great Swap." Hayes carried out his promise and withdrew the remaining troops from the South. Many people in the southern states resented those in the North after their defeat in the Civil War. Hayes wanted to make sure that the southern states were welcomed back into the Union. But this attitude angered the Republican Party, because the Republicans were in favor of harsh penalties against the southern states.

AGAINST CORRUPTION

After the corruption of Ulysses Grant's presidency, Hayes tried to make the government more honest. He stopped the system of appointing friends and party supporters to senior positions. Instead, he introduced a system that was based on ability and not on "who you know." This policy was attacked by both parties, which had always made sure that their own

No. 1
Hayes was the first president to use the telephone, which was invented by Alexander Graham Bell in 1876. His phone number in the White House was 1.

> *He serves his party best who serves his country best.*
>
> **RUTHERFORD HAYES, 1877**

☆ **TERM**
1877–1881

☆ **PARTY**
Republican

☆ **VICE PRESIDENT**
William Wheeler

☆ **FIRST LADY**
Lucy Webb

☆ **STATES IN THE UNION** *38*

19th president

RUTHERFORD HAYES

1822
Born in Delaware, Ohio

1845
Graduates from Harvard Law School

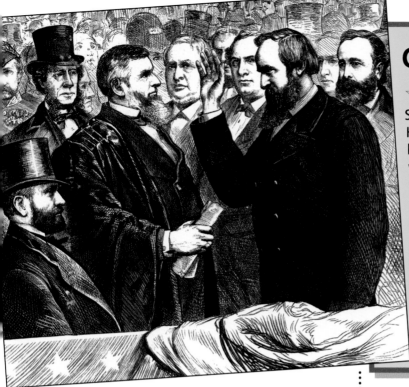

CONTESTED ELECTION

⭐ In the election of 1876, the Democrat Samuel Tilden won 4.3 million votes, and Hayes won 4 million. Tilden beat Hayes by 184 to 165 in the electoral college, which was one short of the total needed for victory. Twenty electoral college votes from three southern states were disputed. The contested election was decided by a special committee of Congress. Hayes promised to remove troops from the occupied southern states. As a result, the committee divided along party lines, and the Republican majority gave all twenty votes to Hayes, who won the election by one electoral vote.

▲Hayes was an honest president, but his presidency was controversial from the day he was sworn into office in 1877. His opponents thought he had won the election by fraud and refused to cooperate with him during his years in office.

supporters received the best government jobs. Hayes was not completely successful in getting rid of corruption. He did, however, have success in firing the powerful New York customs collector and future president, Chester Arthur. He was also successful in improving the nation's finances and providing schooling for African American pupils.

ONE-TERM HAYES

Hayes was made more unpopular as president because his wife never drank alcohol. She was nicknamed "Lemonade Lucy" because she did not serve alcohol in the White House. Hayes always said that he would be president for one term only, and in 1881, he stepped down from office. He returned to Ohio and devoted himself to charitable work until his death.

▶ Lucy Hayes was the first First Lady to have gone to college. She supported equal rights for women, though she thought that women should not vote.

▶ In 1879, Thomas Edison patented the lightbulb.

861
nters U.S.
rmy during
ivil War

1865
Elected to House of Representatives

1868
First elected governor of Ohio

1876
Wins presidential election for Republicans

1877
Ends Reconstruction

1881
Leaves office to do charitable work

1893
Dies in Fremont, Ohio

JAMES GARFIELD

☆ **TERM**
1881

☆ **PARTY**
Republican

☆ **VICE PRESIDENT**
Chester Arthur

☆ **FIRST LADY**
Lucretia Rudolph

☆ **STATES IN THE UNION** *38*

1831
Born in Cuyahoga County, Ohio

1856
Teaches ancient languages and literature

1859
Enters politics in Ohio

> *My God, what is there in this place that a man should ever want to get in it?*

**JAMES GARFIELD
ABOUT THE
WHITE HOUSE, 1881**

James Garfield was only the second president, after Abraham Lincoln, to be assassinated while in office. He was president for less than a year, so he had little chance to leave a mark on the country. Yet James Garfield's life was full of adventure and controversy.

FROM RAGS TO WASHINGTON

James Garfield was born into a poor family on a frontier farm in the state of Ohio. As a youth, he worked as a farmer, canal boatman, and carpenter. He graduated from Williams College in 1856.

In Hiram, Ohio, Garfield was a teacher of ancient languages and literature at the Western Reserve Eclectic Institute, which was later renamed the Hiram Institute. He soon became the principal of the college, while at the same time training as a minister of the church and as a lawyer. In 1859, he was elected to the Ohio state senate as an antislavery candidate. When war broke out in 1861, Garfield joined the Union army, rising to become a major general of volunteers. He left the army in 1863, when he was elected to the House of Representatives.

Garfield was a strong supporter of the Republican Party, and he enforced Reconstruction in the defeated southern states of the Union. Garfield also opposed President Hayes's campaign to wipe out corruption and patronage in the **civil service**. By 1880, Garfield was an important figure in national politics.

What happened next surprised the nation. Garfield went to the Republican Party convention as a campaign manager for Senator John Sherman.

1861
Enlists in the Union Army

1863
Elected to House of Representatives

1880
Wins presidential election for the Republicans

1881
Shot by Charles Guiteau

1881
Dies in Elberon, New Jersey

▶ In a gunfight at the O.K. Corral in Tombstone, Arizona, in 1881, Deputy Marshall Wyatt Earp and his brothers, Virgil and Morgan, gunned down their rivals, the Clanton brothers.

The convention could not decide which candidate to choose. It was split between the Stalwarts, who supported the former president, Ulysses Grant, and the supporters of Congressman James Blaine. Garfield worked hard to stop both candidates from winning the nomination, and after thirty-five ballots, the convention decided to seek a compromise. On the thirty-sixth ballot, Garfield was chosen as candidate. He was known to only a few electors, but he won the nomination.

With a majority of just over 9,000 votes, Garfield was elected president, defeating Democrat, Winfield Hancock, who was a Union war hero.

SHORT TERM

When Garfield became president, his vice president was Chester Arthur, a member of the Stalwarts, while James Blaine became secretary of state. In office, Garfield overturned the anticorruption crusade of former president Rutherford Hayes and used patronage to reward his friends and supporters.

But many people were still upset by the way that Garfield had become president, and on July 2,1881, Charles Guiteau,

a Stalwart who had wanted Chester Arthur to become president instead, shot Garfield.

Garfield survived eleven weeks before he died on September 19. The Stalwarts had won, and Arthur took over as president.

FIRSTS
James Garfield was the first president to campaign in both English and German. He was also the first left-handed president.

▶ Frank Leslie's Illustrated Newspaper of July 1881 pictures Garfield after he has been shot by his assassin, Charles Guiteau.

1829
Born in North Fairfield, Vermont

1854
Becomes a lawyer in New York

1861
Quartermaster general of New York state militia

1865
Helps Republican Party gain power in New York

1871
Customs collector of New York

▶ Mark Twain's famous book, *The Adventures of Huckleberry Finn*, was first published in the United States in 1885.

1878
Removed as customs collector

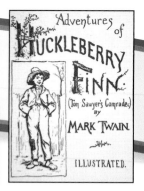

Throughout the presidencies of Grant, Hayes, and Garfield, the topics of patronage and corruption filled U.S. politics. One man summed up these problems perfectly – Chester Arthur.

Arthur, the son of Irish immigrants in Vermont, studied law. When the Republican Party was formed in 1854, he joined immediately and soon became a major figure in New York politics. During the Civil War, he became quartermaster general for New York state. His job was to make sure that essential war supplies were ready for use. Arthur was a hard worker and got along well with people. He used the contacts that he made to help the New York senator Roscoe Conkling build a powerful political organization in the state. In return, Arthur was made customs collector of New York, the busiest and richest port in the country.

CORRUPT POLITICS

Arthur used this post to make both himself and his friends richer. The patronage system worked by making sure that political friends and supporters

☆ **TERM**
1881–1885

☆ **PARTY**
Republican

☆ **VICE PRESIDENT**
None

☆ **FIRST LADY**
None

☆ **STATES IN THE UNION** *38*

21st president

...to gobble all the vacancies for his particular friends, and to talk reform at every gobble.

AN OBSERVER ON ARTHUR'S USE OF PATRONAGE

CHESTER ARTHUR

◄ When the Brooklyn Bridge opened in 1883, many people described it as the Eighth Wonder of the World.

1880
Vice president to James Garfield

1881
Becomes president on Garfield's death

1885
Steps down as president

1886
Dies in New York City

received well-paid and influential jobs in government, which they could use to help advance their patron's political career. Sometimes money changed hands, but more often it was influence that counted. A group of people known as "Conkling's Stalwarts" was the biggest, most influential, and most corrupt organization in Republican politics, and Chester Arthur was at the heart of it.

INTO THE PRESIDENCY

In 1880, the Republicans chose James Garfield as their presidential candidate. The Stalwarts had wanted the former president Ulysses S. Grant as their candidate, but when he lost, they had to settle for Chester Arthur as vice presidential candidate instead. After Garfield was murdered in 1881, Arthur became president. Many were horrified at the prospect, as they feared that Arthur would fill the government with his supporters.

To everyone's surprise, Arthur turned his back on his corrupt ways.

He pledged to get rid of patronage, and did nothing to help his former Stalwart friends. In 1883, he signed the Pendleton Civil Service Reform Act, which set up a civil service based on ability and merit, not on party patronage. Arthur also reformed the post office and other organizations.

As a result, Arthur lost the support of the Stalwarts, and the Republican Party was seriously weakened. In 1884, the party chose his old rival, James Blaine, as its presidential candidate. Arthur became fatally ill and stepped down as president in 1885. He died the following year.

► William Frederick Cody, who was nicknamed Buffalo Bill, first put on his successful *Wild West Show* in 1883.

GROVER CLEVELAND

22nd & 24th president

☆ **TERMS**
1885–1889,
1893–1897

☆ **PARTY**
Democratic

☆ **VICE PRESIDENTS**
Thomas Hendricks,
Adlai Stevenson

☆ **FIRST LADY**
Frances Folsom

☆ **STATES IN
THE UNION** *38, 45*

*Public office is
a public trust.*

CAMPAIGN SLOGAN, 1884

WHITE HOUSE WEDDING
Cleveland was the only president to marry during his term of office. His wife, Frances, was twenty-seven years younger than he was.

Grover Cleveland is the only president in the history of the United States of America to have served two separate terms as president. In the first term, he was successful, but it may have been better if he had not returned for a second term.

MR. CLEAN
Grover Cleveland was the son of a Presbyterian minister. He studied law and opened a practice in Buffalo, New York. He was hardworking, efficient, and honest. These qualities worked to his advantage as a politician. He joined the Democratic Party and, in 1882, made his reputation as mayor of Buffalo. While he was mayor, he stopped corruption and patronage in city government. From there, his political career took off.

The next year, he became a successful governor of New York and continued to fight corruption. In 1884, he was chosen as the presidential candidate for the Democratic Party. His Republican opponent, James Blaine, was linked to this corruption. Because of Cleveland's clean reputation, he became the first Democratic president to be elected since before the Civil War.

1837
Born in Caldwell, New Jersey

1859
Becomes a lawyer in Buffalo, New York

1882
Anticorruption mayor of Buffalo

1883
Governor of New York state

1884
Elected president

1888
Loses to Benjamin Harrison

1892
Regains presidency

1893
Economic slump causes widespread unemployment

MAKING CHANGES

As president, Cleveland continued President Arthur's policy of **reform** of the civil service, but Cleveland was sensible enough to keep those Republicans who were good at their jobs.

High **tariffs** had been in place since the Civil War to raise money for the government. Cleveland lost support from many in his own party when he tried to remove these tariffs. People in business liked the tariffs because they made the rich even richer, but ordinary working people disliked the tariffs because they caused high prices for many goods. In the 1888 presidential election, Republican Benjamin Harrison opposed Cleveland. Harrison favored keeping the tariffs in place. Cleveland won the majority of the popular vote, but he lost the election in the electoral college.

NOT SO POPULAR

Harrison was an unpopular and inefficient president, and in 1892, Cleveland swept back into power. But his second term in office was not successful.

The U.S. economy was in a state of disorder, and many workers were losing their jobs. Violent fights broke out between business owners and workers.

Many of the workers were organized in **trade unions**. The U.S. government sent in federal troops to get the U.S. mail on the move when it was held up because of a rail strike. Many workers were angered by this action and by the other tough measures Cleveland took.

In 1896, the Democratic Party was divided on the subject of how to deal with the **economic depression**, or the slump in the U.S. economy, and Cleveland was not renominated for president. It was the end of his political life.

THE STATUE OF LIBERTY

☆ The world-famous Statue of Liberty was designed by the French sculptor Frédéric Auguste Bartholdi. The statue was built as a monument to freedom. The statue towers 305 ft. (93 m) above the ground and stands on an island in New York City's harbor. The statue was unveiled by President Cleveland on October 28, 1886.

The Statue of Liberty

1897
Steps down from presidency

1908
Dies in Princeton, New Jersey

▲ The American bison was almost extinct by 1893. The picture *The Last of the Buffalo* was painted by Albert Bierstadt in 1888 and helped to save bison from extinction.

BENJAMIN HARRISON

BENJAMIN

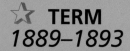

23rd president

⭐ **TERM**
1889–1893

⭐ **PARTY**
Republican

⭐ **VICE PRESIDENT**
Levi Morton

⭐ **FIRST LADY**
Caroline Scott

⭐ **STATES IN
THE UNION** *44*

*Grandfather's Hat
Fits Ben*

CAMPAIGN SLOGAN, 1888

SHOCKING BEHAVIOR

Harrison installed electric lights in the White House but was so scared of electric shocks that he left them on all the time.

Benjamin Harrison is **the only president whose grandfather – William Harrison – was also president.** Harrison's great-grandfather, who was also called Benjamin, had signed the Declaration of Independence, and his father served in the House of Representatives. Politics was in the younger Benjamin Harrison's blood, but when he finally reached the presidency, he achieved little.

As a young man, Harrison trained as a lawyer in Cincinnati before moving to Indianapolis in 1854. For the next twenty-six years, he practiced business law and stopped for only a while during the Civil War, when he led a regiment of volunteers that he had organized himself. Harrison was active in Republican politics, but he failed twice to win the governorship of Indiana. In 1881, he won election to the U.S. Senate but was defeated in 1887. His political life looked to be over.

INTO THE WHITE HOUSE

In 1888, Harrison attended the Republican Party convention. To everyone's surprise, he was chosen as the presidential nominee. He won the election against Grover Cleveland because Harrison said he would keep the tariffs on imported goods as high as possible. His election marked the growing **alliance**

1833
Born in North Bend, Ohio

1852
Graduates from Miami University, Ohio

1854
Moves to Indianapolis and practices law

1862
Commands Indiana volunteer regiment in Civil War

1881
Elected to U.S. Senate

1887
Loses seat in Senate

1888
Wins president election, defeat Cleveland

between big business and the Republican Party. This alliance is still strong in the United States today.

In office, Benjamin Harrison increased tariffs by signing the McKinley Tariff Act, and he took other probusiness measures. But he also signed the Sherman Antitrust Act, which began to control the vast industrial companies that dominated U.S. industry. Harrison also modernized the navy, reformed the civil service, and expanded U.S. naval power in the Pacific Ocean.

▲ To celebrate the 400th anniversary of Columbus reaching the Americas, an international exhibition was held in Chicago, with a giant Ferris wheel measuring 250 ft. (76 m) across.

NATIVE AMERICANS

☆ Ever since arriving in North America during the 1600s, American settlers had fought with Native Americans over land. By the 1880s, the U.S. government had restricted the living area of Native Americans to a few Indian reservations.

One of the final battles between settlers and Indians took place at Wounded Knee Creek in South Dakota around Christmas 1890. The Seventh U.S. Cavalry killed about 150 members of the Sioux Nation. The massacre marked the end of the Indians' fight against rule by the U.S. government.

Ceremonial headdress of a Sioux warrior

CLEVELAND AGAIN

Harrison tried to get reelected in 1892, but the country disliked the high tariffs and big business associated with the Republicans. As a result, Grover Cleveland and the Democratic Party returned to office. Harrison retired from politics and returned to practice law in Indianapolis, where he died in 1901.

1890
Sioux are defeated at Battle of Wounded Knee

1892
Defeated by Cleveland in presidential election

1901
Dies in Indianapolis, Indiana

1843 Born in Niles, Ohio

1861 Serves in Union Army during Civil War

1867 Becomes a lawyer in Ohio

1876 Elected to the House of Representatives

1890 Passes McKinley Tariff Act through Congress

1890 Loses seat as a result of the McKinley bill

1891 Elected governor of Ohio

1896 Wins presidential election

1898 Spanish-American War starts

In the 1770s, American colonists fought for their freedom against the British Empire. Just over a century later, their descendants created their own "American Empire." The president responsible for this huge growth of U.S. power and lands was William McKinley.

Like many presidents, McKinley trained as a lawyer before entering politics as a Republican in 1876. He was a friend of big business executives and in 1890 pushed through Congress the McKinley Tariff Act, which raised a range of taxes on imported goods. But this success lost him his seat in Congress as antitariff Democrats swept to power. McKinley returned to his native Ohio, where he served two terms as governor.

In 1896, McKinley became his party's presidential candidate. His opponent was the Democrat William Bryan, who

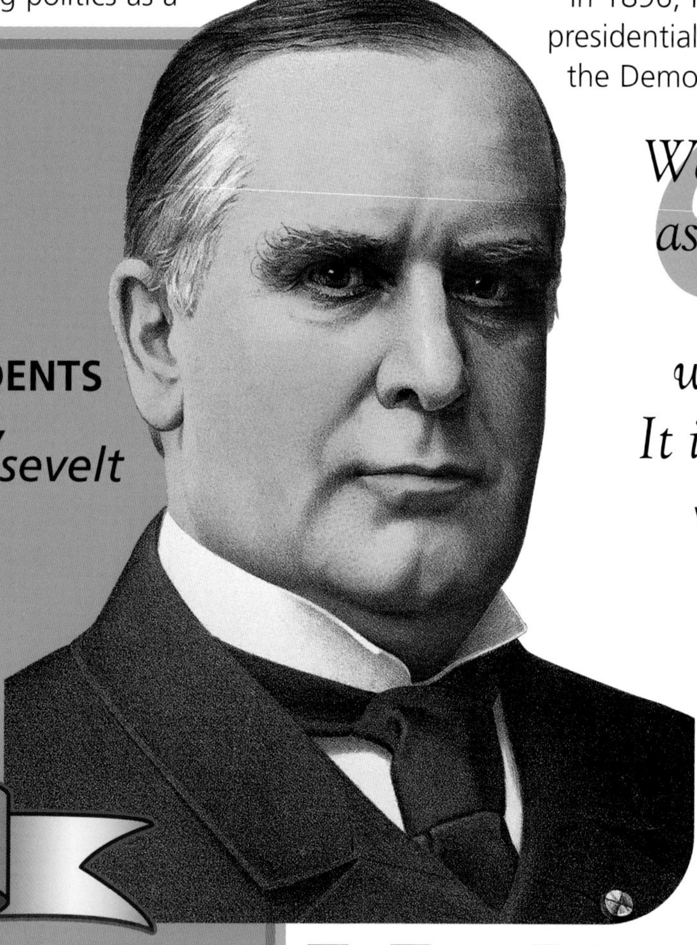

☆ **TERM**
1897–1901

☆ **PARTY**
Republican

☆ **VICE PRESIDENTS**
Garret Hobart, Theodore Roosevelt

☆ **FIRST LADY**
Ida Saxton

☆ **STATES IN THE UNION** *45*

"We need Hawaii just as much and a good deal more than we did California. It is manifest destiny."

WILLIAM MCKINLEY, 1898

THE WHITE WHITE HOUSE
McKinley disliked the color yellow and banned it from the White House. The walls were painted white or another sober color.

25th president

WILLIAM MCKINLEY

▶ Ragtime was the most popular music of the day, and songs like *The Entertainer*, composed by Scott Joplin, sold in the millions.

▶ The shooting of McKinley on September 6, 1901, was reported around the world.

THE PRESIDENT SHOT AT THE EXPOSITION.

1898
Hawaii and other Pacific islands annexed

1900
Wins reelection as president

1901
Assassinated at Pan American Exposition in New York

The U.S. had become a major world power.

McKinley won the 1900 presidential election largely because he was in favor of tariffs and empire-building. His new vice president was Theodore Roosevelt, a hero of the Spanish war.

A few months after McKinley was reelected, he began to change his mind on tariffs. He preferred to work out commercial treaties between nations to lower tariffs and create a market for U.S. exports. He took this message to the Pan American Exposition in New York state in 1901.

At the exposition, a Polish anarchist, Leon Czolgosz, shot McKinley, who died about a week later. He was the third president to be assassinated in office but, unlike his predecessors, his vice president was very able to take over his job.

▲ The 1898 Spanish-American War ended with a U.S. victory. About 400 U.S. soldiers died in battle, though another 4,000 died of disease as America acquired the island of Cuba.

wanted lower taxes to help the country out of an economic depression. McKinley campaigned in favor of tariffs and won with ease.

THE SPANISH-AMERICAN WAR

During the 1890s, the Spanish Empire in the Caribbean and Pacific Ocean was crumbling. Many Americans demanded U.S. intervention to help Cuba in its revolt against Spanish rule, but McKinley refused.

In February 1898, the U.S. battleship *Maine* exploded in Havana Harbor, Cuba. The U.S. government blamed Spain for the explosion and declared war. Within months, Spain was defeated and its Caribbean and Pacific empire taken over by the United States. America also acquired land in Hawaii and Samoa, and U.S. forces crushed a rebellion against European and U.S. control in China.

THE AMERICAN EMPIRE

☆ As a result of the five-month war against Spain in 1898, the United States acquired Puerto Rico, the Philippines, the island of Guam, and Cuba. Spain's empire in the Americas and Pacific Ocean ended.

☆ In the same year, the United States took over Hawaii and in 1899, it divided Samoa with Germany. America had become a major economic power in both the Caribbean Sea and the Pacific Ocean.

THEODORE ROOSEVELT

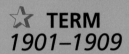
26th president

☆ **TERM**
1901–1909

☆ **PARTY**
Republican

☆ **VICE PRESIDENT**
Charles Fairbanks

☆ **FIRST LADY**
Edith Carow

☆ **STATES IN THE UNION** *46*

> *Speak softly and carry a big stick; you will go far.*
>
> **THEODORE ROOSEVELT, 1901**

MODERN PRESIDENT
While in office, Roosevelt became the first president to go up in an airplane and down in a submarine, the first to visit a foreign country, and the first to ride in a car.

When Theodore Roosevelt became vice president to William McKinley, one fellow Republican stated: "Don't any of you realize that there's only one life between that madman and the presidency?" A few months later, "that madman" became president. Theodore Roosevelt became one of the most remarkable presidents America has ever known.

Roosevelt left Harvard University in 1880 and within two years was elected as a Republican to the New York state assembly. There he made a name for himself because he liked to bring about reform and was not afraid to challenge his own party if he thought he was right. In 1889, Roosevelt was called to Washington to join the Civil Service Commission. He became New York City police commissioner and was very successful at getting rid of corruption. In 1897, Roosevelt returned to the government as assistant navy secretary.

THE ACTION MAN
Roosevelt enjoyed the challenge of war, and as soon as fighting broke out with Spain in 1898, he went to Cuba. He returned a hero and went into political office as governor of New York. He continued to encourage changes in his party's ideas.

1858
Born in New York City

1880
Graduates from Harvard

1882
Elected to New York state assembly

1889
Joins Civil Service Commission in Washington, D.C.

1895
Becomes New York City police commissioner

1897
Assistant navy secretary under McKinley

1898
Leads Rough Riders in Spanish-American War

1898
Becomes governor of New York State

1900
Vice presid under McKinley

◀ Roosevelt was fond of hunting wild animals. But his refusal to kill a bear cub started a craze in toy bears named after him, and the first "Teddy" bears were sold.

Roosevelt attacked big business and corruption and tried to help the poor. Many Republicans did not like his policies and arranged for him to become vice president to McKinley in 1900 to remove Roosevelt from active politics in New York. After McKinley was assassinated, Roosevelt became president.

ATTACKING BIG BUSINESS

Roosevelt was a powerful and energetic president. He fought big business by regulating its activities, so that business was kept under the control of government. He created the Department of Commerce and Labor to regulate industry and set up laws to control the food and drug industries and the railroads. He reorganized the Forest Service and vastly increased the number of national parks and nature reserves. His only failure came when he tried to create a multiracial Republican Party in the southern states. Many members of his own party were against this idea.

In 1903, Colombia rejected the U.S. idea of building a canal across its northern province of Panama in central America. Roosevelt encouraged Panama to fight Colombia and become an independent state, allowing U.S. construction and later control of the Panama Canal.

In 1904, war broke out between Russia and Japan. Roosevelt negotiated a peace treaty between the two countries in 1905 and was awarded the **Nobel Peace Prize**. America was on its way to becoming the richest, most powerful, most important nation on Earth. To show off its strength, Roosevelt sent the U.S. Navy – called the Great White Fleet – on a world cruise starting in 1907.

In 1909, Roosevelt handed the presidency over to William Taft, the successor that he chose himself. But Taft was not happy being president, and in 1912, Roosevelt challenged him for the Republican presidential nomination. Roosevelt lost, so he stood as an independent **progressive candidate.** Some Republican supporters voted for Roosevelt and some for Taft, which split the number of votes for the party. The Democratic Party won the election.

Roosevelt was a modern politician, but his own Republican Party did not support his policies. He left an impression on U.S. politics and government that lasted many years.

THE ROUGH RIDER

☆ Roosevelt gained a reputation in Cuba as an action man during the Spanish-American War, when he commanded his own cavalry regiment, the Rough Riders. They distinguished themselves in the Battle of San Juan Hill, above the important Cuban port of Santiago.

San Juan Hill, Cuba

1904
Wins reelection as president

1906
Wins Nobel Peace Prize

1909
Steps down as president

1912
Fights for the presidency for the Progressive Party

1919
Dies in Oyster Bay, New York

01
omes president
en McKinley is
ssinated

◀ In December 1903, the Wright Brothers became the first people to fly an airplane. They flew over Kitty Hawk, North Carolina.

William Taft didn't really want to be president at all and hated politics. His first and last love was law. After Taft graduated from Yale University, he gained a law degree from a school in his hometown of Cincinnati. A series of jobs in the Ohio state government gained him a good reputation both as a lawyer and as an administrator.

In 1890, he became U.S. **solicitor general** in President Benjamin Harrison's government, and then a circuit judge. In 1898, the United States took over the Philippines. Taft was appointed civil governor of the colony in 1900, bringing it peace.

The people of the Philippines wanted independence, but Taft worked hard to convince them that being part of America was a good thing. He built schools, roads, and irrigation projects and sold land cheaply to poor farmers to help them become richer.

On his return to Washington in 1904, he became secretary of war, and in 1908, Theodore Roosevelt chose him as the Republican presidential candidate.

AN UNHAPPY PRESIDENT

Taft won the 1908 general election by a landslide. He carried on Roosevelt's work against the powerful industrial companies and supported workers and the poor. During his presidency, two changes were made to the Constitution. One of these set a federal income tax. The other allowed senators to be elected by the people for the first time.

But Taft did not enjoy politics – he described the White House as "the lonesomest place in the world" and stated that politics made him sick. Roosevelt turned against Taft and fought him for the Republican presidential nomination in 1912.

> *I would rather be chief justice of the United States, and enjoy a quieter life than that which comes with the White House.*
>
> **WILLIAM TAFT, 1910**

☆ **TERM**
1909–1913

☆ **PARTY**
Republican

☆ **VICE PRESIDENT**
James Sherman

☆ **FIRST LADY**
Helen Herron

☆ **STATES IN THE UNION** *48*

27th president

WILLIAM TAFT

1857
Born in Cincinnati, Ohio

1878
Graduates from Yale University

1880
Gains law degree

STARS AND STRIPES NAILED TO THE NORTH POLE"

DR. FREDERICK A. COOK
APRIL 21 1908.

COMMANDER ROBERT E. PEARY
APRIL 6 1909.

TWO DAUNTLESS AMERICANS WHO REACHED THE GOAL OF A THOUSAND YEARS AND PLANTED THE STARS AND STRIPES UPON THE AXIS OF THE WORLD.

◀ On April 6, 1909, U.S. explorer Robert Peary and his African American companion, Matthew Henson, claimed to be the first people to reach the North Pole. Frederick Cook had made the same claim a year earlier, on April 21, 1908.

When Roosevelt lost the party nomination, he decided to run for president as an Independent, gaining eighty-eight electoral college votes to Taft's eight. The winner of that election, Woodrow Wilson, gained a total of 435 votes.

BACK TO THE LAW

At this point, Taft retired to teach law at Yale University. In 1921, his dream came true when the Republican president, Warren Harding, appointed him chief justice of the U.S. Supreme Court. He

held the job until his death nine years later. During his time as chief justice, Taft proved that he was a cautious but capable judge. He is the only man to have held both the top political and the top legal job in the United States of America, that of president and of Supreme Court chief justice.

▶ On the night of April 14, 1912, the luxury liner *Titanic* was halfway across the North Atlantic Ocean on its first voyage, traveling between England and New York City. The ship struck an iceberg and sank beneath the waves, killing 1,517 people.

THE BIG PRESIDENT

☆ William Taft weighed 332 lb. (150 kg), the heaviest U.S. president in history. But he did not "throw his weight around" while he was president. In fact, he liked to make jokes about his size and was a good-natured man with an infectious chuckle.

890
ecomes
.S. solicitor
neral

1892
Appointed
U.S. judge

1900
Governor of
the Philippines

1904
U.S. secretary
of war

1908
Elected
president

1912
Defeated
by Wilson

1921
Chief justice of
U.S. Supreme
Court

1930
Dies in
Washington,
D.C.

◀ Jack Johnson was the first African American world heavyweight champion. He held the title from 1908–1915.

61

WOODROW WILSON

> *The world must be made safe for democracy.*
>
> **WOODROW WILSON, 1917**

☆ **TERM**
1913–1921

☆ **PARTY**
Democratic

☆ **VICE PRESIDENT**
Thomas Marshall

☆ **FIRST LADIES**
Ellen Axson, Edith Galt

☆ **STATES IN THE UNION** *48*

LAWN GRAZING
During World War I, Wilson kept a flock of sheep at the White House to keep the lawns under control. He liked to wander outside and pat their heads.

Woodrow Wilson had two successful careers. The first, and the longest, was as an academic and a writer of books about politics and government. The second career was as president of a country at war, and this job brought him international fame.

Wilson was a slow learner to begin with and did not make sense of the alphabet until he was nine. He made up for lost time by studying at Princeton University and later gaining a law degree. After a year as a lawyer in Atlanta,

Georgia, he returned to academic life, first at Johns Hopkins University and then at Princeton. He became president of Princeton, where he changed and modernized the way it taught its students. Wilson's work at Princeton influenced university education across America. But he made enemies, too, and in 1910, he resigned.

INTO POLITICS
Wilson then changed careers. He ran as the Democratic candidate for governor of New Jersey and won the election. As governor, he introduced many reforms. These made him famous, and in 1912, he was his party's candidate for president.

Although he had more experience at academic debate, Wilson was a good campaigner.

1856
Born in Staunton, Virginia

1879
Graduates from Princeton University

1882
Qualifies as a lawyer at the University of Virginia

1883
Earns a Ph.D. from Johns Hopkins University

1890
Professor of law and politics at Princeton University

1910
Elected governor of New Jersey

1912
Elected president

1914
World War breaks out in Europe

WORLD WAR I

⭐ War broke out in Europe in 1914, when the heir to the Austrian-Hungarian throne was assassinated. Great Britain, France, Russia, and others were on one side; Germany, Austria-Hungary, and Ottoman Turkey were on the other. In 1917, Germany began attacking U.S. ships to prevent it from supplying Britain with food and other materials. The U.S. government declared war on Germany and sent troops to fight in Europe. The arrival of U.S. troops helped Britain and its allies win the war in 1918.

U.S. troops in Europe in 1918

He promised a "New Freedom," which would improve welfare for poor people and conditions for working people. One opponent, Theodore Roosevelt, promised a "New Nationalism," and President Taft's Republican policies offered no change. Wilson won the election with ease.

Wilson lowered tariffs to encourage trade and set the first federal income tax to raise money for the government. He supported the trade unions and made strikes legal. He also approved the Adamson Act, which meant that railroad workers could not be forced to work more than eight hours a day. Other workers then gained the same privilege. Wilson also restricted the use of children as workers in factories and mines.

THE PEACEMAKER

As president, Wilson was a campaigner for peace. He tried to keep America out of overseas battles and avoided war with Mexico, which was in the middle of a violent revolution. When Germany sank the ocean liner *Lusitania* in 1915, killing more than 100 U.S. citizens, Wilson refused to go to war. In 1916, he was reelected, and in 1917, he was forced to join World War I when Germany attacked U.S. ships in the Atlantic Ocean.

After the war with Germany, Wilson worked hard to create a lasting peace. In 1918, he proposed a world peace treaty called the Fourteen Points and suggested that an international organization be formed to help settle arguments between countries. It was called the **League of Nations**. In 1920, Wilson received the Nobel Peace Prize for his peacekeeping efforts. But in the same year, the U.S. Senate refused to agree to the treaty or to allow the U.S. to join the league. This was a serious defeat for Wilson, and he retired from the presidency a broken man.

▶ The world's first jazz record was made in 1917. Soon, jazz music was very popular in the United States. Most jazz bands originated in New Orleans.

World War I recruitment poster

1916 Reelected president

1917 U.S. enters World War I

1918 Sets out Fourteen Points

1920 Wins Nobel Peace Prize

1921 Steps down as president

1924 Dies in Washington, D.C.

▶ The Model T Ford was the first mass-produced U.S. car. By the 1920s, it could be seen all over America.

Warren Harding is said to be at the top of everyone's list of the worst U.S. presidents. He became president almost by accident, and as president, he was surrounded by scandal. Few people mourned his early death.

LUCKY BREAK

Harding was born in Ohio, and after attending a local college, he held a number of different jobs. During this time, he failed to become a lawyer, sold insurance too cheaply and was fired, taught school and hated it, sold hardware, played the cornet in a band, and ended up as a journalist.

His wife, Florence, was very ambitious, and she encouraged him to follow a political career. He was elected as a Republican to the Ohio state assembly and, in 1915, got to the U.S. Senate, where he did not achieve very much. Warren Harding's big break came during World War I. He proposed a congressional bill that would have allowed Theodore Roosevelt, the former president, to raise a volunteer army. The bill did not become law, but Roosevelt appreciated Harding's support and asked him to be his running mate in the next presidential election. When Roosevelt died suddenly, Harding won the presidential nomination himself and was elected president in 1920.

THE GAMBLER
Harding played poker in the White House and gambled away some of its china. He also drank bootleg liquor, even though it was banned.

THE SCANDALOUS YEARS

After the war years, Americans wanted a return to normality, or "normalcy" as Harding called it. Harding took advantage of this wish, stating that he and Florence were "just plain folks." He won

> *...we must strive for normalcy to reach stability.*

WARREN HARDING, 1921

☆ **TERM**
1921–1923

☆ **PARTY**
Republican

☆ **VICE PRESIDENT**
Calvin Coolidge

☆ **FIRST LADY**
Florence De Wolfe

☆ **STATES IN THE UNION** *48*

29th president

WARREN HARDING

1865
Born in Corsica, Ohio

1880
Studies at Ohio Central College

1884
Becomes partner in the *Marion Star* newspaper

◀ The scandal over the Teapot Dome oilfield in Wyoming revealed a high level of corruption in the Harding government. After a Senate investigation into the event, many politicians were forced to resign.

POLITICS.

By permission of]   [The Minneapolis Journal.
THE POT IS BEGINNING TO BOIL.

U.S. CONGRESS.

the election by a landslide. But once Harding became president, his lack of ability was discovered. "I know how far removed from greatness I am," he stated. He proved that this statement was true, as he did little good as president. He did not like to get involved in problems unless it was absolutely necessary. His policies supported big business and high tariffs. This was a complete change from the **interventionist** approach of both Theodore Roosevelt and Woodrow Wilson. Harding was not a good manager, and he appointed some corrupt people to his government.

This move proved to be fatal for some of those involved. In 1923, two of his colleagues killed themselves when rumors spread about their behavior. As Harding toured the United States, a huge scandal broke out. Some of his cabinet members had taken money from oil companies in exchange for allowing the companies to exploit the Teapot Dome oilfield. Soon afterward, Harding collapsed and died, leaving other people to fix these problems.

PROHIBITION

⭐ In 1919, the manufacture, sale, import, and export of alcohol was banned in America. This was known as Prohibition, because any contact with alcoholic drink was prohibited. Gallons of alcohol were poured away. These laws were established by the Eighteenth Amendment to the Constitution, which introduced Prohibition and stayed in place until 1933. Many people ignored Prohibition and openly disobeyed the law. People drank alcohol in illegal bars called "speakeasies." Gangsters got rich by importing illegal alcohol, known as bootleg liquor. In the end, Prohibition failed, because instead of decreasing the drinking of alcohol, it increased crime.

Bootleg liquor is emptied into the gutter.

This is the great picture upon which the famous comedian has worked a whole year.
6 reels of Joy.
Charlie Chaplin in "THE KID"

1891
Marries Florence De Wolfe

1899
Elected to Ohio state assembly

1903
Lieutenant governor of Ohio

1910
Fails to be elected governor

1915
Elected to U.S. Senate

1920
Elected president

1923
Dies in San Francisco, California

▶ The 1920s was the age of the silent picture. Millions of people went to the movies to see stars such as Charlie Chaplin (left).

1872
Born in Plymouth, Vermont

1897
Becomes a lawyer

1899
Elected to Northampton city council in Massachusetts

1907
Elected to Massachusetts state assembly

1910
Elected mayor of Northampton

1918
Elected governor of Massachusetts

Although he was a man of few words, Calvin Coolidge became famous when he made a statement as governor of Massachusetts in 1919. When the Boston police force went on strike, Coolidge sent in the state militia to crush the strike. "There is no right to strike against the public safety by anybody, anywhere, any time," he said. His words were heard and appreciated across the nation, and his Republican Party chose him as vice presidential candidate to Warren Harding. When President Harding died unexpectedly in 1923, Coolidge was sworn in as the new president.

IN HIS OWN LIGHT

Like many other presidents, Coolidge trained as a lawyer and worked in city and state politics first, ending up as Massachusetts governor. When Harding died, Coolidge's father administered the presidential oath of office by lantern light at his Vermont home. Coolidge came to Washington, D.C., determined to end the corruption of Harding's cabinet and win his own reelection.

The chief business of the American people is business.

CALVIN COOLIDGE, 1925

☆ **TERM**
1923–1929

☆ **PARTY**
Republican

☆ **VICE PRESIDENT**
Charles Dawes

☆ **FIRST LADY**
Grace Goodhue

☆ **STATES IN THE UNION** *48*

30th president

A DARK HORSE

Calvin Coolidge was not as quiet as he seemed. He kept a pet racoon and rode an electric rocking horse most days, whooping like a cowboy.

CALVIN COOLIDGE

► In 1929, the first Academy Award was given by the Academy of Motion Picture Arts and Sciences.

1920
Elected vice president to Warren Harding

1923
Becomes president on death of Harding

1924
Wins reelection as president

1929
Steps down from the White House

1933
Dies in Northampton, Massachusetts

◄ In 1927, Charles Lindbergh was the first person to fly single-handedly across the Atlantic Ocean. His flight from New York City to Paris, France, took 33 hours, 29 minutes.

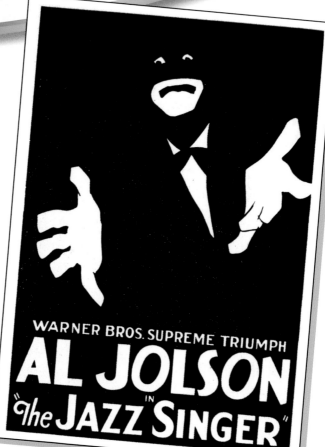

A LIGHT TOUCH

Coolidge was a typical conservative Republican. He believed in letting business get on with the business of making money, and he opposed government aid to poor farmers or anyone else. He preached that the less the government got involved, the better for everyone. The country was getting very rich after World War I, and Coolidge just allowed it to get richer, keeping quietly out of the way.

He reduced taxes and the **national debt**, encouraged people to invest in the stock exchange, and worked hard for peace abroad. But in the next decade, some of these decisions turned out to be the wrong ones for the United States.

At the time, however, Coolidge easily won the presidential election of 1924 and may have won again in 1928 if he had wanted to carry on as president. Instead, he announced his retirement from politics and settled down to write a book about his life. He died peacefully in his hometown of Northampton, Massachusetts.

▲ The world's first talking picture appeared in October 1927. *The Jazz Singer* starred Al Jolson and included spoken words for the first time. Until then, moviegoers could hear only sound effects and background music.

THE SILENT ONE

☆ Coolidge hardly spoke, and when he did, he said only a few words. He was nicknamed "Silent Cal," and when he died, American writer Dorothy Parker remarked: "How do they know?" A number of other people are said to have made the same comment.

HERBERT HOOVER

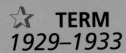

31st president

⭐ **TERM**
1929–1933

⭐ **PARTY**
Republican

⭐ **VICE PRESIDENT**
Charles Curtis

⭐ **FIRST LADY**
Lou Henry

⭐ **STATES IN THE UNION** *48*

> *...we shall soon ...be in sight of the day when poverty will be banished from this Nation.*
>
> **HERBERT HOOVER, 1928**

THE WESTERNER
Herbert Hoover was the first president to be born west of the Mississippi River. He was also the first Quaker to be president.

Herbert Hoover was **one of the best-qualified men to become president. He had worked** hard and become a millionaire, and he was very good at administration. He also had been successful in government. Unfortunately, his period in office coincided with the greatest economic depression in American history, and Hoover did not manage this crisis well.

Hoover began with little in life. His parents died before he was nine, and he was brought up by his uncle – a Quaker doctor – and his aunt in Oregon. He left high school at age fourteen to work as an office boy. He later became interested in engineering and graduated from Stanford University with a degree in mining engineering. In 1908, he set up his own mining consulting company, which made him very rich.

In 1914, Hoover was in London, England, when World War I began in Europe. He chaired the American Relief Commission (ARC), which helped the 150,000 Americans caught in the war to return home safely. When America entered the war in 1917, Hoover ran several American organizations that helped victims of war and sent food to the millions of people in Russia who did not have enough to eat.

1874
Born in West Branch, Iowa

1895
Graduates from Stanford University

1914
Becomes chair of American Relief Committee

1917
Becomes U.S. food administrator

1921
Secretary of commerce under Harding, then Coolidge

1928
Elected president

1929
Great Depression begins

▲The New York Stock Exchange on Wall Street in New York City was the world's busiest stock market. Investors bought and sold stocks in U.S. companies, receiving a dividend, or share of the profits, when the company did well.

INTO GOVERNMENT

Hoover's work during the war brought him to the attention of President Harding, who made him **secretary of commerce**. He continued to hold this post under President Coolidge. In this job, Hoover worked with companies to set safety standards for workers and safety rules for automobiles and railroads. He also helped the new airlines to get started. Hoover began a series of building projects, including the Boulder Dam, which was later renamed the Hoover Dam in his honor.

Hoover was the natural choice to succeed Calvin Coolidge as president. He promised prosperity for all and believed the richness of the 1920s would continue forever. The Wall Street stock market crash ended such dreams.

1932
Loses presidential election to Roosevelt

1947, 1953
Heads Hoover Commissions into government reform

1964
Dies in New York City

◀ The Empire State Building, the world's tallest skyscraper at that time, opened in New York City in May 1931. It is 1,250 ft. (380 m) tall and has eighty-six floors.

Hoover did not like the government to take too much control. He took little action to solve the problem other than to cut taxes and encourage business in the hope that the **Great Depression** would solve itself. It did not. Many people blamed Hoover because they were unemployed and poor. As a result, he became extremely unpopular.

A NEW CAREER

Hoover eventually realized that something had to be done to stop the depression, so he set up an organization to help industry. This turned out to be too little, too late, and Franklin Roosevelt beat Hoover in the presidential election of 1932.

Hoover retired from public life. Then in 1946, he once again organized food supplies to war victims in Europe. In 1947 and again in 1953, he headed the federal Hoover Commissions. These groups helped the government manage the United States, which was rich and powerful after World War II.

THE GREAT DEPRESSION

☆ During the 1920s, the value of company shares rose steadily on the New York Stock Exchange, and Americans became wealthy. Then, on October 29, 1929, the stock market crashed. Share prices, and therefore the value of U.S. companies and goods, fell heavily. As a result, the U.S. economy collapsed, and by 1933, America was producing half what it did in 1929. By 1933, during the Great Depression, about 13 million people were unemployed (one in four of the working population). Farmers lost their land, people lost their savings, and the nation was in ruins.

Unemployed people line up for free food.

1882
Born in Hyde
Park, New York

1904
Graduates from
Harvard University

1910
Elected to the
New York Senate

1913
Assistant secretary
of the navy under
President Wilson

1920
Runs as
vice presidential
candidate but
loses election

1921
Contracts
polio

1928
Elected governor
of New York

◄ In the 1930s farms in the Midwest were lost under dust blown by strong winds. The area was known as the Dust Bowl.

FREE TIME
To relax from the pressures of work, Roosevelt liked to organize his collection of 25,000 postage stamps, which he had collected into forty albums.

In a time of great need, as millions of Americans lost their jobs and homes, the country elected an outstanding president.

Franklin Roosevelt served longer than any other U.S. president, including his distant relative, Theodore Roosevelt. He brought hope to millions of people and helped the nation through the Great Depression and World War II.

Roosevelt practiced as a lawyer, but he realized that he was more interested in politics. He became active in the Democratic Party and was elected to the New York state senate in 1910. President Wilson made him assistant secretary of the navy in 1913, a position that he held throughout the war. In 1920, he was the vice presidential candidate to James Cox, but the men lost to Republicans Warren Harding and Calvin Coolidge. Despite this defeat, Roosevelt's future looked promising. But in 1921, polio disabled him, and he was confined to a wheelchair.

☆ **TERM**
1933–1945

☆ **PARTY**
Democratic

☆ **VICE PRESIDENTS**
*John Garner,
Henry Wallace,
Harry Truman*

☆ **FIRST LADY**
Eleanor Roosevelt

☆ **STATES IN
THE UNION** *48*

32nd president

"...the only thing we have to fear is fear itself."

**INAUGURAL
ADDRESS, 1933**

FRANKLIN ROOSEVELT

▶ U.S. and Allied troops land on the French coast on D-Day, June 6, 1944.

1936, 1940
Reelected president

1941
America enters World War II

1944
Reelected president

1945
Dies in Warm Springs, Georgia

FEISTY FIRST LADY

Eleanor Roosevelt, the niece of President Theodore Roosevelt, was as famous as her husband. She wanted to help poor people and those who were badly treated, and helped to write the Universal Declaration of Human Rights in 1948.

Many people thought his public life would be over, but Roosevelt disagreed. He fought back and won election as governor of New York in 1928. He was a good administrator and introduced many popular reforms in the state. In 1932, he ran for president. As the Great Depression got worse, Roosevelt promised to make the people of America rich once again. He called this "the new deal for the American people." This promise helped him to defeat President Hoover in the presidential election by a landslide victory.

THE NEW DEAL

At his inauguration in 1933, Roosevelt stated that the only thing the country had to fear was "fear itself." He was very active, and within ninety-nine days of

WORLD WAR II

In 1939, Nazi Germany invaded Poland, so Great Britain and France declared war on Germany. World War II broke out in Europe. At first, the United States did not take sides in the war, although it agreed to lend Britain ships and other military equipment. In return, Britain let the United States use some of its military bases. On December 7, 1941, Japanese airplanes bombed the U.S. naval base Pearl Harbor, in Hawaii. This forced the U.S. government to declare war on Japan and Germany. Millions of Americans fought in the war alongside British and Russians, until Germany and Japan were defeated in 1945.

becoming president, he had made major reforms in U.S. government. These changes, known as the **New Deal**, set America on the road to recovery. The financial and economic systems were transformed. The poor were given assistance, the elderly received pensions for the first time, and programs were provided to help the unemployed find work. Not all Roosevelt's measures worked, but they gave the American people new hope for the future.

WORLD LEADER

Throughout his presidency, Roosevelt spoke to his nation on the radio in regular "fireside chats." These talks reassured people and made Roosevelt very popular. As a result of this popularity, Roosevelt was reelected president a total of three times.

During the war, Roosevelt played a major role in supporting the army and reassuring the American people. Along with Winston Churchill of Great Britain and Josef Stalin of Russia, Roosevelt planned for the future of the world after the war had ended. But because Roosevelt got so heavily involved in world events, his hard work started to harm his health. In April 1945, Roosevelt died suddenly, very close to the end of the war. On his death, Americans knew that they had seen a time when one of the most remarkable men who ever lived had been their president.

Japan attacks Pearl Harbor.

1884
Born in Lamar, Missouri

1906
Takes over family farm

1917
Enters army during World War I

1934
Elected to Senate

1944
Chosen as vice president by Roosevelt

1945
Becomes president on Roosevelt's death

1945
United States drops two atomic bombs on Japan to end war

▶ The world's first atomic bomb was dropped on the Japanese city of Hiroshima on August 6, 1945.

To most people, Harry Truman did not seem like a potential president. But when Truman took over from Roosevelt in 1945, he surprised the world with his ability and skill as leader of the country.

Harry Truman was born on a farm in Missouri. He did not go to college, but he held a number of jobs before he took over the farm's management. During World War I, he enlisted in the army and fought in France.

On his return from France, he married Bess Wallace and opened a men's clothing store. The store failed, so in 1922 he became a Democratic politician in Missouri. He was an honest and hard-working politician, and in 1934, Truman was elected to the U.S. Senate.

Truman was a good senator. In 1941, he was appointed chair of a committee that reviewed America's national defense. The committee's suggestions saved huge sums of money and improved the production of war materials. It was a great success and became known as the Truman Committee.

> *The buck stops here!*
>
> **MOTTO ON TRUMAN'S DESK**

☆ **TERM**
1945–1953

☆ **PARTY**
Democratic

☆ **VICE PRESIDENT**
Alben Barkley

☆ **FIRST LADY**
Bess Wallace

☆ **STATES IN THE UNION** *48*

33rd president

THE SILENT "S"
Harry Truman's middle initial was "S." The letter did not stand for any name, but both his grandfathers thought he was named after them!

HARRY TRUMAN

The United Nations, formed 1945 by the nations fighting Germany and Japan in World War II, helps all countries to work for world peace.

948
ns second
m as president

1950
Sends U.S. troops to fight in Korea

1953
Steps down as president

1972
Dies in Kansas City, Missouri

NOT A GOOD START

⭐ Truman was clever enough to go to college, but did not because his father, a farmer, had no money. Truman's poor eyesight meant that he could not go to military academy either. He spent his childhood playing the piano and wanted to be a concert pianist, but his parents could not afford to pay for lessons. As president, he had three pianos in the White House.

▲Almost every American expected Harry Truman to lose the 1948 presidential election, and one newspaper – the *Chicago Daily Tribune* – even put a headline on the front page saying he was defeated. In fact, Truman won the election with ease.

Truman was chosen by Roosevelt as his vice presidential running mate in 1944. Truman did not get along well with Roosevelt, but nonetheless, they won the election. Then, after eighty-two days, Roosevelt died, so Truman took over the top job.

SURPRISE PRESIDENT

At the time, World War II was still being fought. The war with Germany was almost over, but the war with Japan continued. One of Truman's first jobs as president was to decide whether to drop two atomic bombs on the Japanese cities of Hiroshima and Nagasaki. He chose to use the bombs and brought the war to an end in 1945.

Truman dealt quickly with the problems of the postwar world. He promised U.S. aid to war-torn Europe and countries fighting **Communism**.

Truman passed laws to stop **racial discrimination** against African Americans. The United States was in a period of expansion, full employment, and growing prosperity. In 1948, Truman decided to seek reelection as president. Two candidates from his own party opposed him. These were the pro-discrimination South Carolina governor, Strom Thurmond, and Roosevelt's former vice president, Henry Wallace. The Republicans were expected to win. But, to everyone's surprise, Truman was elected to a second term.

A NEW VIEW

America and the Soviet Union had been on the same side in World War II, but by the end of the 1940s, they were rivals. The two never had any physical battles but did fight a **Cold War** in Europe, Asia, and Africa. In 1949, Truman led the United States into the **North Atlantic Treaty Organization (NATO)**, which tied America and Western Europe together for security against Soviet-dominated Eastern Europe. In 1950, he sent U.S. troops to fight in the war that broke out when Communist North Korea invaded U.S.-backed South Korea.

By the time Truman left office in 1953, most people had changed their view of the president. He had been dismissed as "a little man," but many realized that he was tougher and far cleverer than they had thought. In getting the United States through all its difficulties after 1945, Truman proved himself to be just as capable and far-sighted as his much-admired predecessor, Franklin Roosevelt.

DWIGHT EISENHOWER

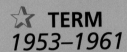

34th president

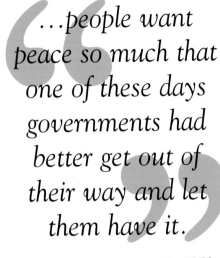

⭐ **TERM**
1953–1961

⭐ **PARTY**
Republican

⭐ **VICE PRESIDENT**
Richard Nixon

⭐ **FIRST LADY**
Mamie Doud

⭐ **STATES IN THE UNION** *50*

> *...people want peace so much that one of these days governments had better get out of their way and let them have it.*

DWIGHT EISENHOWER, 1959

CAMP DAVID

Dwight Eisenhower was devoted to his grandson, David. Eisenhower renamed Shangri-la, the presidential retreat in Maryland, Camp David, in his honor.

Like many presidents before him, Dwight Eisenhower was a wartime hero who became president. And like them, he was first and foremost a soldier. His politics were conservative and cautious, and he could have fit into either political party. He appeared casual, but his appearance hid a strong ambition.

Eisenhower was born in Texas, but at age two, his family moved to Kansas. He attended West Point military academy, where he played football until an injury stopped him. He stayed in the United States during World War I, training tank battalions. His career really took off when he graduated first out of a class of 275 from the Command and General Staff School at Fort Leavenworth, Kansas. From then on, his progress was rapid. By June 1942, six months after the United States had entered World War II, Eisenhower beat 366 senior army officers to become commanding general of U.S. forces in Europe. In that job, he organized Operation Overlord – the campaign to free Europe from Nazi Germany. In June 1944, he commanded the largest seaborne invasion in history, the **D-Day Landings** on the Normandy beaches in France.

1890
Born in Denison, Texas

1915
Graduates from U.S. Military Academy at West Point, New York

1932
Becomes aide to General Douglas MacArthur, U.S. Army chief of staff

1941
Promoted to brigadier general

1942
Commander, U.S. forces in Europe

1944
Leads D-Day invasion

1945
Becomes army chief of staff

POSTWAR SERVICE

By now Ike, as he was commonly known, was famous. He was not a daring leader, but he attracted loyalty from his troops and was good at keeping control of the U.S., French, and British generals who reported to him.

When the war ended in 1945, Eisenhower wanted to retire, but instead he was made army chief of staff. Eisenhower oversaw the task of reorganizing the vast army for peace. In 1948, he left the army to become president of Columbia University in New York. But in 1949, Ike was back in the army, as head of the new North Atlantic Treaty Organization (NATO).

WAR AND PEACE

At this point, Eisenhower considered a career in politics. Both political parties approached him to be their candidate for the election. In 1952, he ran for the Republican Party's nomination. He won on the first ballot and, in November 1952, was elected president.

THE SPACE RACE

⭐ In 1957, the Soviet Union sent the world's first artificial satellite into space. It was called *Sputnik I*. In 1961, the Soviets sent the first astronaut into space. The first person to walk on the Moon was the American Neil Armstrong, in 1969.

Yuri Gagarin, the first man in space

EASY-GOING IKE

⭐ The Eisenhowers moved house thirty-five times in the first thirty-five years of their marriage, but Mamie Eisenhower never complained. "I have only one career, and his name is Ike," she said.

General "Ike" Eisenhower

⭐ Ike took up oil painting as a good way to relax and be alone. He enjoyed golf so much that the U.S. Golf Association built a hole for him near the White House.

Eisenhower promised to go to Korea to break the deadlock in the war, and a truce was signed in July 1953.

There were growing racial problems in America at this time. African Americans were demanding their **civil rights**. Eisenhower ended **segregation** in education but did little else to support civil rights.

The rivalry between the Soviet Union and the United States continued. Eisenhower increased the number of U.S. nuclear weapons and ensured that his country kept a stronger army and more weapons than the Russians. The launch by the Soviets of the world's first satellite in space in 1957 was a severe blow to America, which wanted to be the first country to do this.

America struggled to deal with the age of nuclear weapons and Soviet power. But Eisenhower's firm yet friendly leadership and his relaxed style reassured the American people that all was well in the world and that the United States was still strong.

950
pointed
preme
mmander
NATO

1952
Elected
president

1956
Reelected
president

1959
Alaska and
Hawaii join
the Union

1961
Steps down from
the White House

1969
Dies in
Washington,
D.C.

▲ Senator Joseph McCarthy led an aggressive investigation of suspected American Communists in the 1950s.

▲ Elvis Presley's first number one record helped make rock-and-roll music popular in the 1950s.

John Fitzgerald Kennedy was a hugely popular leader, even though he was president for less than three years. He was the first U.S. president born in the twentieth century and one of the youngest ever elected. He was also handsome, with a glamorous wife and a young family. In the years since his death, his reputation has declined. But in the early 1960s, John F. Kennedy was the hope of the world.

Kennedy was born into a large Catholic family. His father, Joseph Kennedy, was once ambassador to Great Britain and was determined that one of his children would become president. John attended Harvard University, then joined the U.S. Navy. As captain of a torpedo boat, he saved his crew when it was sunk by the Japanese in 1943. He was honored for his bravery.

After the war, he entered politics as a Democrat. By 1956, he was well enough known to win his party's vice presidential nomination. Four years later, he won his party's nomination for president. He beat the Republican, Richard Nixon, and became the thirty-fifth president of the United States.

A TIME OF CONFLICT

As president, Kennedy governed a nation torn apart over civil rights. He set out a program that he called the New Frontier, which would tackle poverty and inequality. He made laws to protect people's civil rights, set up medical care for the aged, and spent money on education. He also promised to get an American on the moon by the end of the

> *...ask not what your country can do for you – ask what you can do for your country.*

JOHN KENNEDY, 1961

☆ **TERM**
1961–1963

☆ **PARTY**
Democratic

☆ **VICE PRESIDENT**
Lyndon Johnson

☆ **FIRST LADY**
Jacqueline Bouvier

☆ **STATES IN THE UNION** *50*

35th president

JOHN KENNEDY

CAMELOT
Kennedy surrounded himself with so many glamorous people that the White House was sometimes compared to Camelot, the court of the mythical English King, Arthur, and his knights of the Round Table.

1917
Born in Brookline, Massachusetts

1940
Graduates from Harvard Universi

decade. Congress blocked many of these reforms, but Kennedy gained huge support for his work from African Americans and the poor. In 1962, the Soviet Union placed nuclear missiles on the Caribbean island of Cuba, only a few miles off the U.S. coast. Kennedy ordered the Soviets to remove them. For more than a week, neither country backed down. Then the Soviets gave in. The world had come very close to nuclear war.

In 1963, Kennedy signed a treaty with the Soviets, banning the testing of nuclear weapons in the atmosphere. Tension between the two countries continued, however, as Kennedy sent support to South Vietnam to stop the country from being invaded by **Communist** North Vietnam.

WHAT IF?

By 1963, Kennedy was one of the most popular presidents in history. Then, on November 22, he was shot and killed while visiting Dallas, Texas. The country deeply mourned the loss of their beloved leader. Yet in the years since his death, Kennedy's role in starting the war in

▼America and the Soviet Union came close to nuclear war in 1962. Here, Kennedy inspects U.S. weapons.

CIVIL RIGHTS

☆ John Kennedy supported U.S. civil rights. Although the Constitution stated that African Americans had the same rights as white Americans, many still suffered discrimination. From the mid-1950s, African Americans demonstrated for their civil rights. They held meetings, marched in the streets, and took their case to the courts. The leader of the civil rights movement was a Baptist minister, Martin Luther King, Jr. His nonviolent campaigns made him a popular figure throughout the world.

Vietnam, his many affairs, and his links to gangsters have tarnished his image. Still, two of his brothers have run for president, and the love affair between America and the Kennedy family seems to continue.

THE ASSASSINATION

☆ On November 22, 1963, Kennedy visited Dallas with his wife. Traveling in an open-top car, he was shot dead. Lee Harvey Oswald, a former U.S. Marine, was arrested for the crime, but two days later he was shot in jail by Jack Ruby, a local nightclub owner. The new president, Lyndon Johnson, set up the Warren Commission to find out if Oswald had acted alone or if there had been a conspiracy to kill Kennedy. The commission stated that Oswald alone had killed the president, but many theories still exist about who actually killed JFK.

News that shocked the world

CHICAGO DAILY NEWS

PRESIDENT IS KILLED

Texas Sniper Escapes; Johnson Sworn In

941
ns
S. Navy

1946
Elected to House of Representatives

1952
Elected to Senate

1956
Fails to become Democratic vice presidential candidate

1960
Elected president

1962
Confronts Russia over missiles in Cuba

1963
Assassinated in Dallas, Texas

77

LYNDON JOHNSON

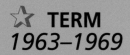

36th president

⭐ **TERM**
1963–1969

⭐ **PARTY**
Democratic

⭐ **VICE PRESIDENT**
Hubert Humphrey

⭐ **FIRST LADY**
Claudia "Lady Bird" Alta Taylor

⭐ **STATES IN THE UNION** *50*

> *This administration, today, here and now, declares unconditional war on poverty in America.*
>
> **LYNDON JOHNSON, 1964**

LBJ x 5
Every member of Lyndon Baines Johnson's family shared his initials: his wife Lady Bird, his daughters, Lynda Bird and Luci Baines, and even the family dog, Little Beagle.

Lyndon Johnson's **presidency is one of the great tragedies of U.S. history. Johnson had not** expected to become president. He made many important changes to the way the country was run and he supported the poor and disadvantaged. But a war divided his country and lost him his job.

Lyndon Johnson was a Texan who trained as a teacher and taught for two years before working for a Texas congressman. In 1935, President Roosevelt made Johnson head of the New Deal National Youth Administration in Texas. By 1937, Johnson was in the House of Representatives. Eleven years later, he was elected to the Senate.

Johnson was committed to the ideals of Roosevelt's New Deal and pushed through many new laws. He led the fight for the 1957 and 1960 civil rights acts and supported social **welfare** and other programs that helped the less fortunate in society. Johnson was also good at fixing political and social problems. As a result, he was the Democratic **minority leader** in the Senate in 1953, the **majority leader** in 1955, and then his party's presidential candidate. He lost to John Kennedy, and became his vice president when Kennedy won the

1908
Born near Stonewall, Texas

1930
Graduates from Southwest Texas State Teachers College

1937
Elected to House of Representatives

1948
Elected to Senate

1953
Becomes Democratic leader in the Senate

1960
Runs for the presidency, and becomes vice president to Kennedy

1963
Becomes presid[ent] after assassinat[ion] of Kennedy

election. About three years later, Kennedy was assassinated, and Lyndon Johnson became the president of a saddened nation.

Johnson grabbed the opportunity to push changes through Congress. In 1964, Congress became overwhelmingly Democrat, which helped Johnson to get his new laws passed. He introduced Medicare – government-funded health care for the elderly – and the important Civil Rights Act and Voting Rights Act. He gave money to education and the arts, raised the **minimum wage**, and introduced laws to protect consumers and the environment. These reforms aimed to get rid of

▲ Johnson is sworn in as president as Jacqueline Kennedy (right) watches. They were aboard the plane carrying John Kennedy's body back to Washington after his assassination.

THE VIETNAM WAR

☆ In 1954, the former French colony of Vietnam was divided between a Communist North and a pro-American South. North Vietnamese soldiers entered the south to take over the government and make the country Communist. President Kennedy sent the first U.S. military advisers to South Vietnam in 1961. In 1964, Johnson asked Congress for permission to wage war in Vietnam. Nearly 400,000 U.S. soldiers were in Vietnam by 1966, and U.S. planes were dropping bombs on North Vietnam daily. America eventually realized it was not going to win the war. It withdrew U.S. troops and signed a cease-fire in 1973.

poverty in the richest country in the world. Many Americans came to prosper in Johnson's new society. In 1964, Johnson ran for president and won the election with one of the biggest landslides in history.

VIETNAM

Johnson believed that Communism was a threat to the world. He sent thousands of soldiers to South Vietnam to prevent a Communist takeover. As the Vietnam War continued and the deaths mounted, people started to protest. Johnson's "Great Society" was soon overshadowed by the horrors of Vietnam. In 1968, Johnson was so unpopular with the American people that he decided not to run for president a second time and retired.

Five years later Johnson died, exhausted and disappointed that his reputation as a great reformer had been destroyed by a war he could not win.

1964
Sends troops to Vietnam

1964
Wins presidential election

1964
Civil Rights Act passed

1965
Voting Rights Act passed

1968
Announces he will not run again for president

1973
Dies near San Antonio, Texas

Civil rights leader Martin Luther King, Jr. inspired people with his speeches. He was assassinated in 1968.

1913
Born in
Yorba Linda,
California

1937
Gains law degree
from Duke
University

1942
Joins
U.S. Navy

1946
Elected to House
of Representatives

1950
Elected
to Senate

1952
Vice president
to Eisenhower

1960
Loses presidential
election to
John Kennedy

1962
Loses election
for governor
of California

Richard Nixon is the first and only president who resigned while in office. He was distrusted and disliked before he became president and was disliked even more afterward. He was, in many ways, a successful president, but his dishonesty let him down.

Nixon was born in California and became a lawyer. After war service, he ran for the House of Representatives. Nixon claimed that one of the Democrats in the House supported Communism. Nixon won his place by promising to fight Communists. He then became a member of the **House Un-American Activities Committee (HUAC)** and became famous for his prosecution of the supposed Communist spy Alger Hiss.

In 1950, Nixon ran for the Senate. He criticized his opponent, Helen Douglas, and won again. Dwight Eisenhower chose Nixon as his vice presidential running mate. But Nixon was charged with using campaign funds for himself during his Senate race, and he won only by appealing on television for support from the public. Nixon turned out to be a better vice president than many people had imagined. He supported civil rights but also wanted to increase

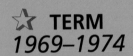

☆ **TERM**
1969–1974

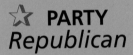

☆ **PARTY**
Republican

☆ **VICE PRESIDENTS**
*Spiro Agnew,
Gerald Ford*

☆ **FIRST LADY**
Thelma "Pat" Ryan

☆ **STATES IN THE UNION** *50*

37th president

RICHARD NIXON

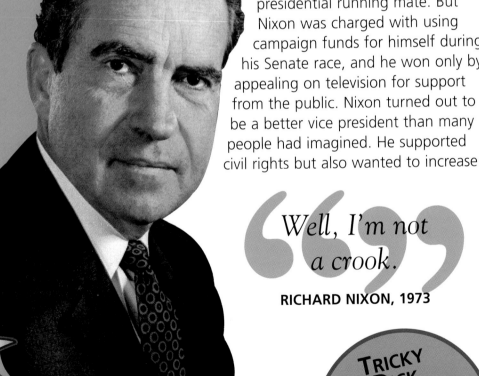

*Well, I'm not
a crook.*

RICHARD NIXON, 1973

TRICKY DICK
Throughout his career, people had doubts about Richard Nixon's honesty. Long before Watergate, he was known as "Tricky Dick" Nixon.

◀ In 1972, President Nixon made a historic visit to China, the first ever by a sitting U.S. president.

1968
Elected president

1969
Apollo 11 lands on the moon

1972
Break-in at the Democratic HQ, Watergate Hotel

1972
Reelected president

1973
Cease-fire ends U.S. involvement in Vietnam War

I WANT OUT

1974
Resigns because of Watergate involvement

1994
Dies in New York City

◀ There were many U.S. protests against the Vietnam War in the early 1970s.

America's influence abroad. When Eisenhower stepped down in 1960, Nixon fought John Kennedy for the presidency. He lost narrowly and then fought and lost an election to become governor of California. "You won't have Nixon to kick around anymore," he snarled at the press, and many thought that his political career was over.

IN AND OUT OF POWER

But Nixon's career was not over. He rebuilt his reputation and, in 1968, narrowly won the presidential election. As president, he cut spending and introduced anticrime measures. In 1972, he signed a treaty with the Soviet Union to reduce the number of weapons the two countries held. Nixon also withdrew U.S. troops from Vietnam and turned the army into a volunteer force.

But Nixon trusted no one except his closest advisers. Throughout his time in office, he used his power to bully people and bug telephones. Nixon was so keen to win reelection in 1972 that he used unfair and illegal means to slander the Democratic Party. These activities were made public when it was revealed that Nixon had secretly taped all his

▲ On July 20, 1969, Neil Armstrong became the first person to walk on the moon. He said it was "one small step for a man, one giant leap for mankind."

conversations in the White House. The evidence on the tapes ruined him. By this time, many of his advisers – including Vice President Agnew – had resigned in disgrace or faced criminal charges. Nixon himself faced a huge bill for unpaid taxes.

Faced with all this, Nixon resigned rather than face impeachment by Congress. Nixon may not have been the first president to use dirty tricks against his opponents, but he was the first to get caught. This scandal, along with his bad reputation, meant that he left government in disgrace.

WATERGATE

☆ In June 1972, burglars broke into the headquarters of the Democratic National Committee at the Watergate Hotel in Washington, D.C. They were part of a secret plan to keep the Democrats from winning the 1972 election. Evidence soon emerged that this plan had been run from the White House. Many of Nixon's advisers were forced to resign. Nixon himself resigned in disgrace in August 1974.

Nixon announces his resignation.

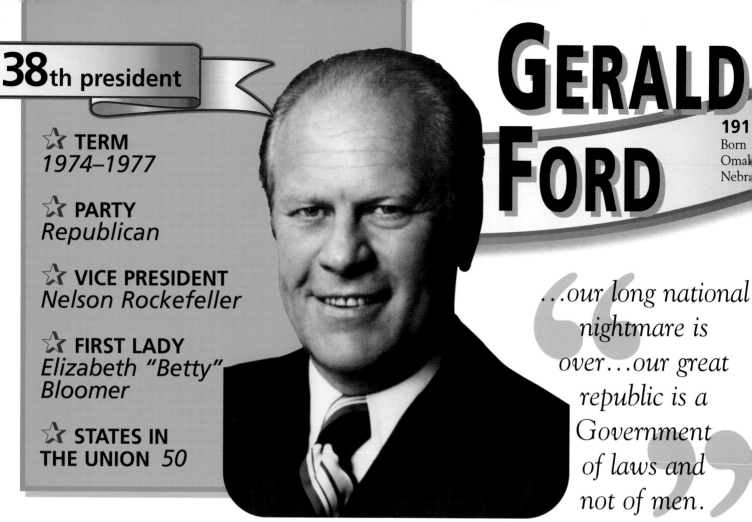

GERALD FORD

191
Born
Omal
Nebr:

★ **TERM**
1974–1977

★ **PARTY**
Republican

★ **VICE PRESIDENT**
Nelson Rockefeller

★ **FIRST LADY**
Elizabeth "Betty" Bloomer

★ **STATES IN THE UNION** *50*

"...our long national nightmare is over...our great republic is a Government of laws and not of men."

GERALD FORD, 1974

Gerald Ford became president because of the resignation of Richard Nixon. **No one elected Ford to be president, just** as no one had previously elected him to be vice president. He was the only person in U.S. history to hold both offices without being elected to either. His time in office was short and unmemorable.

UNELECTED OFFICE

Ford was a keen sportsman who practiced law and served in the U.S. Navy during World War II before entering politics in 1948. For fifteen years, he was a competent Republican member of the House of Representatives. In 1965, Ford became the minority leader in the House for the Republican Party. He might have stayed in this post, but in 1973, Spiro Agnew was caught taking bribes and evading taxes, so he was forced to resign as vice president. Nixon chose Ford to take over the job, and Congress approved it. Americans did not vote on the matter.

THE FORDS

★ Gerald Rudolph Ford, Jr. was born Leslie Lynch King, Jr. When he was one year old, his mother divorced his violent father and later married a man called Gerald Rudolph Ford. Leslie Lynch King was later renamed, becoming the second Gerald Rudolph Ford. Ford did not learn about this renaming until he was in his teenage years.

★ Betty Ford was often outspoken. She publicized her breast cancer to help save other people's lives. She also told the world that she was addicted to alcohol and pain-killers, and she set up the Betty Ford Clinic to help people overcome their addictions.

1931
Wins football
scholarship
to Michigan
University

1935
Sports coach at
Yale University

1941
Gains law
degree
from Yale

1942
Joins
U.S. Navy

1948
Elected to
House of
Representatives

1965
Becomes
minority
leader of
the House

1973
Becomes
vice president

1974
Becomes
president
when Nixon
resigns

1976
Defeated in
presidential
election by
Jimmy Carter

◄ President Ford pardons Richard Nixon on U.S. television in 1974.

LEFT AND RIGHT
Gerald Ford is left-handed when he sits down to eat or write, but is right-handed when he stands up to play sports.

By this time, President Nixon was losing popularity because of the growing number of allegations against him of corruption and dirty tricks. Nixon wanted a decent, competent person to be his vice president. Gerald Ford was the perfect man – he was loyal to Nixon but, above all, he was honest and reasonably efficient. Eight months later, Nixon resigned, and Ford became president.

CLEANING UP THE MESS
Ford took over the presidency when the United States was experiencing many problems. The government was full of corruption, and few people had any respect for it or its politicians. The country was still divided after the Vietnam War and, in addition, it was suffering from a massive economic depression and high unemployment. Ford had an advantage because he was well liked and he was obviously a decent person, but he had little political experience for such a high position in government. As he said when he was sworn in as vice president in 1973, "I am a Ford, not a Lincoln." It was unlikely that he could fix all the nation's problems as Abraham Lincoln had tried to do during the Civil War.

Ford's first act as president was to pardon Nixon, which meant that Nixon would not have to face any criminal charges. Ford believed that the country should put the past behind it and look to the future, but many people were furious that Nixon was not being made to face justice for his crimes.

SOME SUCCESSES
Ford did have some successes as president. He continued Nixon's policy of cooperation with the Soviet Union, and he met with its leader, Leonid Brezhnev. Ford also managed to get the remaining U.S. citizens out of South Vietnam without loss of life when the country was finally taken over by North Vietnam in 1975. He also took military action against Cambodia after it seized a U.S. ship. But people still considered him tarnished by his association with Richard Nixon.

Ford won his party's nomination to fight the 1976 election, but he was defeated by Jimmy Carter. This new man promised a different style of politics.

▶ The last American citizens and their families still living in South Vietnam at the end of the Vietnam War are evacuated from the roof of the U.S. embassy in Saigon, the South Vietnam capital, in 1975.

James "Jimmy" Carter was new to politics when he became president. He had never been vice president, or a member of either of the houses of Congress, unlike most of his predecessors. The fact that Carter was new helped him win, but this inexperience also contributed to his lack of success in office.

Carter came from the Deep South, and he was the first president from that region since the Mexican War. He earned his money in the peanut business, and as a Democrat, he rose through Georgia politics to become governor from 1971 to 1975. By law, Carter could only serve one term as governor, so once he was out of office, he turned his attention to the presidency.

Few took him seriously, but Carter offered a style of politics that was almost antipolitics. He was religious, sincere, and honest and was not tainted in any way by the politics of Washington, D.C. In a close race with Gerald Ford, he won the 1976 election and arrived in Washington determined to make a change.

CHANGE IN THE WHITE HOUSE

Carter immediately reorganized the government. He set up the post of energy secretary to deal with the U.S. energy crisis and pardoned the many men who had broken the law by refusing to fight in the Vietnam War. Abroad, he negotiated a treaty with Panama to return the U.S.-controlled Panama Canal Zone to Panama's control by 2000. Carter also established good relations with China and continued to talk with the Soviet Union's representatives about reducing the number of nuclear weapons in the two countries. Above all, he achieved what many thought was impossible by bringing

> ...at the end of this administration we shall be able to stand up anywhere in the world...and say "I'm a Georgian" – and be proud of it.

JIMMY CARTER, 1971

☆ **TERM**
1977–1981

☆ **PARTY**
Democratic

☆ **VICE PRESIDENT**
Walter Mondale

☆ **FIRST LADY**
Rosalynn Smith

☆ **STATES IN THE UNION** *50*

39th **president**

JAMES CARTER

1924
Born in Plains, Georgia

1946
Graduates from U.S. Naval Academy in Annapolis, Maryland

▲ In 1978, President Carter brought Menachem Begin of Israel (left) and Anwar Sadat of Egypt (right) together for peace talks. Since the foundation of Israel in 1948, the country had been in conflict with its Arab neighbors.

THE CARTER TEAM

⭐ Jimmy Carter was a relaxed president. At his inauguration, he got out of his car and walked some of the way to the White House in a show of openness. Jimmy and his wife, Rosalynn, were a real team. She shared all his work problems. Every Thursday, they met for lunch to talk about the decisions that the president had to make in the next week.

together the leaders of Egypt and Israel, countries at war with each other. After serious discussions, the two countries signed the Camp David Accords, and Egypt agreed to recognize Israel in return for regaining its lost region of Sinai. A peace treaty between the two countries was signed in 1979. The Egyptian president, Anwar Sadat, and the Israeli prime minister, Menachem Begin, won the Nobel Peace Prize for this historic reconciliation.

AN ULTIMATE FAILURE

In other aspects of his job, Carter struggled. He was unknown in politics, so he found it difficult to get new laws through Congress. Unemployment and prices rose, and people did not believe Carter could solve the country's economic problems.

In November 1979, a situation arose that ruined Carter's reputation. Iranian soldiers seized the U.S. embassy in the country's capital city of Tehran and held fifty-two U.S. citizens hostage. The following year, a secret U.S. mission failed to rescue them. For many Americans, it was a huge national shame that the strongest country in the world was being held for ransom by a religious group in the Middle East. The Soviet invasion of Afghanistan in late 1979 added to the feeling that the United States was losing its power in the world. As a result, Carter lost the 1980 presidential election by a landslide to the Republican Ronald Reagan, who promised to restore American pride.

After leaving the White House, Carter retired to Georgia. But, unlike other former presidents, he did not leave politics. He uses his political experience to promote world peace. He acts as a negotiator between countries that are at war. He has also overseen elections in newly democratic countries and promoted human rights wherever he can. Over time, his reputation has grown, so that he is now more widely respected than he ever was as president.

▶ In 1978, Muhammad Ali won the world heavyweight boxing championship for a record third time. He had won the title in 1964 and again in 1974.

READ THIS
The president's youngest child, Amy, was invited to state banquets in the White House. She was allowed to bring a book to read during the boring parts.

1953
Leaves U.S. Navy to run father's peanut farm

1962
Elected to Georgia State Senate

1970
Elected governor of Georgia

1976
Elected president

1979
Israel and Egypt sign peace treaty

1980
Loses presidential election to Ronald Reagan

1981
Devotes himself to humanitarian causes

At age sixty-nine, Ronald Reagan was the oldest man to have been elected president. He was also the only president who had been divorced, the leader of a trade union, and a former film star. Reagan was one of the more successful U.S. presidents, despite the many problems that arose during his presidency.

Ronald Reagan was born into a poor family in Illinois. As a teenager, he worked as a lifeguard during the summer, and later became a radio announcer. In 1937, Reagan was noticed by a Hollywood agent who took him to California, where he soon became a film star. Over the years, he featured in more than fifty movies. He became an important member of the Screen Actors Guild (SAG), the trade union for actors, and he was the organization's president six times.

Reagan had grown up during the Great Depression and was a committed Democrat who believed in President Roosevelt's New Deal. But during the 1950s, he began to change his views. Reagan disliked the violence that he saw during a strike at the Warner Brothers studios and believed that Communists were influencing the movie industry. He thought that the Democratic Party was soft on Communism, so he became a Republican in 1962.

A RAPID ASCENT

In 1964, Reagan made a powerful speech in favor of Barry Goldwater, the Republican candidate for president. Goldwater lost the election to Lyndon Johnson, but Reagan still made his reputation with his presentation skills. Two years later, he ran for governor of California and won easily. He promised to cut taxes, reduce government spending, and get tough on student protesters. In reality, his words were tougher than his policies, but he was a successful governor and served for two terms. In 1968 and 1976, Reagan used his popularity to run for his party's presidential nomination. He finally won in 1980.

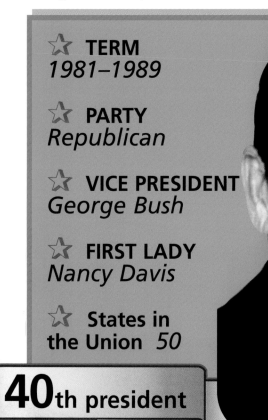

☆ **TERM**
1981–1989

☆ **PARTY**
Republican

☆ **VICE PRESIDENT**
George Bush

☆ **FIRST LADY**
Nancy Davis

☆ **States in the Union** *50*

40th president

TWO MRS. REAGANS
Ronald Reagan is the only president to have been divorced. In 1949, he divorced his first wife, the actress Jane Wyman, to marry another actress, Nancy Davis.

RONALD REAGAN

1911
Born in Tampico, Illinois

1937
Appears in first Hollywood film

1947
Becomes president of the Screen Actors Guild

◀ Ronald Reagan was devoted to his second wife, Nancy, and consulted her on many issues. After he became sick with Alzheimer's disease, Nancy nursed her husband devotedly.

As president, Ronald Reagan offered the American people a new era of confidence in their country. He cut taxes and welfare spending. He also cut down the amount of government money spent on the environment and on civil rights. Reagan spent a lot of money on the armed services and weapons. This policy, known as "Reaganomics," cut **inflation** and unemployment and made the rich richer. But it also made the poor poorer and increased the government's debt to more than $200 billion, which was the highest it had been in U.S. history.

Economically, Reagan's policy was not a great success, but it did revive the American people's confidence in their country and government. It also provided Reagan with a landslide victory when he ran for president again in 1984.

THE SECOND TERM

Reagan worked with the new Soviet leader, Mikhail Gorbachev, to improve relations between the two countries. The two leaders met for talks four times and agreed to destroy some of their nuclear missiles. This was the first time that the number of nuclear weapons in the world had been reduced.

But then Reagan got involved in selling weapons to Iran. He did this to persuade Iran to put pressure on Islamic militants to release hostages that they were holding prisoner in Lebanon. He had previously called Iran one of the most "evil and murderous nations in the world."

SOVIETS VS. AMERICA

⭐ Reagan feared a Soviet attack against the United States, so he updated U.S. defenses. Under Reagan, America began to develop the Strategic Defense Initiative (SDI), known as "Star Wars." This was a kind of shield in space, made from lasers that were meant to destroy missiles coming toward the United States.

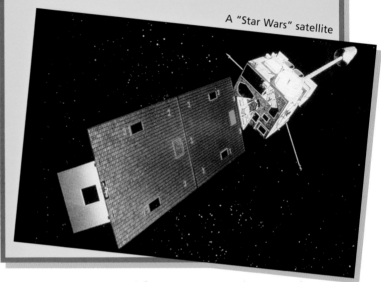

A "Star Wars" satellite

The money gained from Iran was then used illegally. It was given to revolutionaries who were trying to bring down the left-wing government of Nicaragua. When this information became known, Reagan's reputation was severely damaged.

In 1989, Reagan stepped down as president. He left the United States richer and more confident than before, but he also left it with its biggest debt. Many people still think Reagan is one of the most successful and likeable presidents in recent U.S. history.

◀ In 1981, the world's first reusable space shuttle flew back to Earth after fifty-four hours in space.

1962
Joins Republican Party

1966
Elected governor of California

1968, 1976
Attempts to win nomination for presidency

1980
Elected president

1984
Reelected in biggest electoral victory in history

1989
Steps down as president

2004
Dies of Alzheimer's disease complications

▶ Reagan's term saw the start of the computer age. Millions of homes now have computers.

GEORGE BUSH

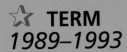

41st president

- ⭐ **TERM**
  1989–1993

- ⭐ **PARTY**
  Republican

- ⭐ **VICE PRESIDENT**
  Dan Quayle

- ⭐ **FIRST LADY**
  Barbara Pierce

- ⭐ **STATES IN THE UNION** *50*

FIRST BASE STAR
George Bush was the captain of Yale's baseball team and played first base. He was good enough to be approached by a professional team and later kept his baseball glove in a drawer in the Oval Office.

> *Read my lips – no new taxes.*
>
> **GEORGE BUSH, 1988**

Few presidents have been as qualified as George Bush to become president. He had been in the armed forces, worked in industry, served as a U.S. ambassador, run the Central Intelligence Agency (CIA), and for eight years was vice president. His term saw worldwide successes, but his failures in the United States meant he lasted only one term.

Bush was born into a rich Republican family and he had a privileged upbringing. His father was a U.S. senator from Connecticut. As soon as he was eighteen, Bush joined the navy and became the then-youngest navy pilot in World War II, flying fifty-eight missions. During one of these missions, he was shot down over the Pacific Ocean. Bush was rescued by a U.S. submarine and received the Distinguished Flying Cross for his bravery. After the war, he studied law at Yale University. Bush then moved to Texas, where he set up a profitable oil development company.

INTO POLITICS

In 1966, Bush was elected to the House of Representatives, serving two terms. When he lost office in 1970, President Nixon appointed him U.S. ambassador to the United Nations (UN), and then chair of the Republican Party. Later, President Ford sent Bush to Communist China – the first U.S. representative posted there. On his return to America, Bush ran the CIA. He was a major Republican figure.

1924
Born in Milton, Massachusetts

1942
Joins navy, serves as fighter pilot in World War II

1948
Graduates from Yale University

1950
Sets up Texas oil development company

1966
Elected to U.S. House of Representatives

1971
U.S. ambassador to the UN

1973
Chairs Republican Party

◀ Barbara Pierce supported her husband's career and has moved with him to seventeen different cities and twenty-nine homes during their long and happy marriage.

In 1980, Bush lost the party's presidential nomination to Ronald Reagan. Bush became vice president and, for eight years, was a loyal supporter.

PRESIDENT AT LAST

In 1988, Bush got his chance. Reagan's second term ended, and Bush was elected president against the Democrat Michael Dukakis. The campaign was one of the toughest in U.S. history.

While Bush was in office, the Cold War came to an end. The Soviet Union withdrew its troops from Afghanistan, which it had invaded in 1979, as well as from Eastern Europe. This allowed many revolutions to take place across the region. Communist governments were overthrown, the Berlin Wall came down, democratic elections were held for the first time, and East and West Germany were united as one country. In 1991, the Soviet Union collapsed, and fifteen new countries were created. Also in 1991, the United States won a victory over Iraq and ended the Gulf War. As a result, Bush became one of the most popular presidents in history.

Although he achieved much abroad, Bush was less successful at home. When he was elected, he had promised not to raise taxes, but he was forced to increase a range of taxes in 1990 to reduce the government's debt. At the same time, unemployment rose and the economy slowed down. Many people were also concerned that America was losing its powerful place in the world economy to Japan and other strong countries. Bill Clinton, Bush's Democratic challenger in 1992, used these fears about the weakness of the U.S. economy to fight hard against Bush. Clinton won the presidential election. After only one term in office, Bush had been defeated.

THE GULF WAR

☆ On August 2, 1990, Iraqi troops invaded their small neighboring country of Kuwait. Iraq wanted to capture this oil-rich country and gain better access to the Persian Gulf. The United States and twenty-eight other countries sent troops into the region to defend Kuwait. On January 17, 1991, U.S. and other air forces began to bomb Baghdad, the Iraqi capital. The land invasion of Kuwait began on February 24. Four days later, Iraq was defeated and Kuwait was free.

U.S. troops in the first Gulf War

1974
U.S. ambassador to China

1976
Director of the CIA

1980
Seeks, but loses, presidential nomination to Reagan

1980
Becomes U.S. vice president under Reagan

1988
Elected president

1991
Sends U.S. troops to the Persian Gulf

1992
Loses presidential election to Bill Clinton

▶ The fall of the Berlin Wall in 1989 united the city of Berlin and led to the unification of Germany in 1990.

1946
Born in Hope, Arkansas

1968
Graduates from Georgetown University

1973
Gains law degree from Yale University

1976
Elected Arkansas attorney general

1978
Elected governor of Arkansas

1980
Loses governorship in election

1982
Regains Arkansas governorship

At age forty-six, Bill Clinton was one of the youngest men elected president. During his two terms, the U.S. economy was buoyant, but political failures and personal scandals marked his presidency.

Bill Clinton was born William Jefferson Blythe. His father died before he was born, and his mother raised him. She remarried, and Bill took his stepfather's last name, Clinton.

Clinton was brilliant at Georgetown University, at Oxford University in Great Britain, and at Yale University, gaining two degrees. He then returned to his home state of Arkansas to enter politics.

Clinton was determined to become president. In 1974, he tried for a seat in the House of Representatives, but failed. Two years later, he was elected attorney general of Arkansas. In 1978, at age thirty-two, he was elected governor, the youngest in the state's history.

☆ **TERM**
1993–2001

☆ **PARTY**
Democratic

☆ **VICE PRESIDENT**
Al Gore

☆ **FIRST LADY**
Hillary Rodham

☆ **STATES IN THE UNION** *50*

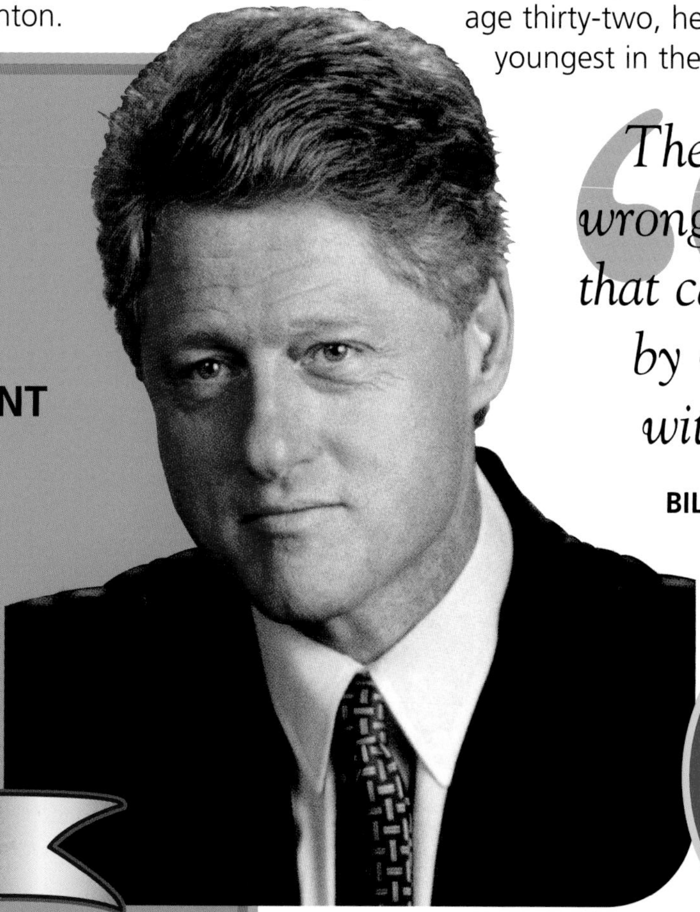

"There is nothing wrong with America that cannot be cured by what is right with America."

BILL CLINTON, 1993

NICKNAMES
Bill Clinton revived his political career so many times after facing defeat that he was known as "the Comeback Kid." He was also known as "Slick Willie," since he could argue both sides of an issue.

42nd president

WILLIAM CLINTON

◄ Clinton worked hard for peace in Northern Ireland.

◄ Clinton worked with Israeli and Palestinian leaders to bring peace to the Middle East.

1992
Wins presidential election for Democrats

1996
Wins reelection

1999
Survives impeachment by Congress

2001
Steps down as president

THE COMEBACK

After one term in office as governor, Clinton was not reelected. He learned the lessons of this defeat and was reelected in 1982, serving five more terms. In 1992, he ran for president as a New Democrat and easily defeated George Bush. Clinton's social policies were in line with the Democrats, but his support of big businesses and small government was more like that of the Republicans.

SUCCESSES AND FAILURES

As president, Clinton was fortunate that the U.S. economy was in good shape. He presided over the longest economic boom in U.S. history. More people had jobs than ever before, and new computer companies made many people rich. As a result, Clinton easily won reelection in 1996.

Clinton had many successes as president. But then he tried to reform the health care system

IMPEACHMENT?

☆ Bill Clinton was the first president since Andrew Johnson in 1868 to face impeachment. In 1998, Clinton was accused of improper behavior. He denied the allegations at first. But after a federal grand jury made an investigation, the special prosecutor, Kenneth Starr, recommended impeachment. The House of Representatives decided that Clinton was guilty of obstruction of justice and perjury (lying in court). The Senate disagreed and acquitted Clinton of the charges in 1999. Clinton was allowed to remain president.

FIRST LADY OF POLITICS

☆ Many people thought that Hillary Rodham would run for president herself, but she chose instead to support Bill in his political

career. In 2000, she decided to run for election as senator for New York state. This was the first time in U.S. history that a First Lady ran for elected office.

to provide good health coverage for all Americans. First Lady Hillary Rodham Clinton promoted the plan, but Congress defeated it. Then, for the first time since 1954, the Democrats lost control of both houses of Congress to the Republicans. Clinton had to abandon many of his own policies and work with a hostile Congress. The two sides had many battles, which Clinton usually won. Then in 1998, Congress impeached him for lying about his relationship with a White House intern, but the "Comeback Kid" survived even that ordeal.

Bill Clinton was a controversial president who attracted respect and hostility in equal measure. Despite the scandals that surrounded him, he ended his two terms as popular as ever, with the United States richer than at any time in its history.

GEORGE W. BUSH

43rd president

☆ **TERM**
2001–

☆ **PARTY**
Republican

☆ **VICE PRESIDENT**
Dick Cheney

☆ **FIRST LADY**
Laura Welch

☆ **STATES IN THE UNION** *50*

> *We will not tire, we will not falter, and we will not fail.*
>
> **GEORGE W. BUSH, 2001**

BUSH DYNASTY

George W. Bush's election was only the second time in history that the son of a president was elected president. John Adams was president from 1797 to 1801. His son, John Quincy Adams, was president from 1825 to 1829.

The younger Bush followed his father into politics and served as governor of Texas for six years.

George W. Bush likely will be remembered as a wartime president. Campaigning as a "compassionate conservative," he began his administration during a time of peace and prosperity. Terrorist attacks soon shattered that feeling of American well-being.

THE POLITICAL LIFE
Bush's grandfather, Prescott Bush, was a well-known Connecticut senator. Bush's father, George H. W. Bush, held several political positions, including U.S. congressman, vice president, and president.

CONTROVERSIAL ELECTION
Bush began to campaign for the presidency in 1999 and won the nomination of the Republican party. He chose Dick Cheney as his running mate. Bush's Democratic opponents were Al Gore and Joe Lieberman.

The Bush-Gore race was close. Whoever won Florida's electoral votes would win the election. When Florida's votes were counted, Bush had won by fewer than 2,000 votes. Even after recounts, the victory in Florida – and the United States – still went to Bush. He was inaugurated in January 2001.

1946
Born in New Haven, Connecticut

1968
Graduates from Yale University

1975
Graduates from Harvard Business School

1977
Marries Laura Welch

1989
Acquires part ownership in the Texas Rangers baseball team

1994
Elected governor of Texas

2000
Elected U.S. president

2001
Largest terrorist attack takes place on U.S. soil

WARTIME PRESIDENT

As Bush took office, the United States had a relatively strong economy. Bush wanted to cut taxes, reform education, strengthen Social Security, and build up the military.

On September 11, 2001, terrorist attacks by the Al Qaeda group changed everything. (See box below.) The attacks caused Bush to launch a "war on terrorism," aimed at Al Qaeda and its leader, Osama Bin Laden, which operated out of Afghanistan. A U.S.-led military invasion of Afghanistan toppled the Taliban government and paved the way for peaceful elections there. Bin Laden was not captured.

Bush cited the war on terror, as well as suspicion that Iraq held weapons of mass destruction (WMDs), as reasons for invading Iraq in March 2003. He believed Iraqi leader Saddam Hussein was preparing to provide these weapons to Al Qaeda or other terrorist groups. Major combat lasted until May 1, although bombings and other attacks by Hussein's supporters continued. U.S. marines captured Hussein in December 2003.

◄ Thousands of people protest the war in Iraq.

In 2004, Bush admitted that Iraq had not been holding WMDs after all. This sparked major protests against the Iraq war, in the United States and around the world. However, Bush insisted that bringing Democracy to Iraq had made the war worthwhile. In January 2005, national elections were held in Iraq to elect a new government, although rebel attacks continued to kill both civilians and soldiers.

REELECTION

Bush ran for reelection in 2004. His opponent this time was Massachusetts senator John Kerry. The election turned on questions of moral character and the ability to lead during crisis. Bush won both the popular and electoral vote. He promised to continue the war on terror.

▶ George and Laura Bush greet supporters after Bush's reelection.

9/11

☆ On September 11, 2001, terrorists hijacked four U.S. airplanes. One plane crashed into a Pennsylvania field, leaving no survivors. Another plane crashed into the Pentagon, in Washington, D.C. Two others crashed into the twin towers of the World Trade Center in New York City, causing them to collapse. The attacks killed over 3,000 people. This one day changed life in the United States. For several days after the attacks, all U.S. air traffic was halted and stock markets were closed.

Since then, security at airports, public buildings, and landmarks has become tighter. Several government safety agencies have combined to form the Department of Homeland Security. And Americans are more aware of the threat of terrorism.

2001
International military coalition invades Afghanistan

2002
U.S.-led troops invade Iraq

2004
Reelected U.S. president

GLOSSARY

abolitionist A person who wants to get rid of slavery.

alliance A partnership between two or more organizations or countries.

ambassador A senior official of one country who represents that country abroad.

American Revolution *See Revolutionary War.*

attorney general The chief law officer in the government who advises the president and cabinet on legal matters.

ballot The act of voting where people mark crosses on paper to choose a party for election.

bill A proposal in Congress for a new law. Once a bill becomes law, it is known as an act.

cabinet The group of officials appointed by the president to run the country.

campaign Speeches, meetings, and other events held before an election to raise support to get a person elected.

civil rights The personal rights of individual citizens in most countries, upheld by law.

civil service The government organization that administers public services in a country.

Civil War The war that broke out in America in 1861 when eleven slaveowning states left the Union.

Cold War The confrontation between America and the Communist Soviet Union for world domination after 1945.

Communism The belief in a society without social class in which the community owns all property.

Communist A person who supports Communism.

Confederacy The eleven southern states that left the Union before the Civil War.

Confederates Those who lived in the southern states during the Civil War. They had their own congress at that time.

Congress The U.S. legislative, or lawmaking, body. It is made up of the Senate and the House of Representatives.

Constitution A written document that sets out the political principles on which a country is founded and how its people are to be governed.

Constitutional Convention The meeting of politicians in 1787 during which the U.S. Constitution was written.

Contintental Army The army of the thirteen colonies that fought for independence from Britain from 1775 to 1783.

Continental Congress The independent government of the thirteen colonies that fought against the British and issued the Declaration of Independence in 1776. It first met in 1774 and was replaced by the U.S. Congress in 1789.

convention The meeting of a political party held every four years to nominate its presidential and vice presidential candidates.

D-Day Landings The U.S.-led invasion of German-occupied France in 1944 that led to the end of World War II in 1945.

Declaration of Independence The declaration made on July 4, 1776, by the thirteen British colonies in North America that they were free from Britain.

delegate A person chosen or elected to represent their town, state, or political party at a conference or meeting.

Democrat A supporter of the Democratic Party.

Democratic Party A political party that first emerged under Andrew Jackson. It is one of the big U.S. political parties today.

Democratic-Republican The party of Thomas Jefferson, which believed in more power to individual states and a limited role for the federal government.

depression *See economic depression.*

diplomat A person who represents a government.

economic depression An economic slump, or downturn in a country's wealth.

electoral college The system of election that is used to elect the U.S. president. *See page 7.*

establishment A group of politicians, business executives, and others who run a country.

federal A system of government where power is shared between national and state governments, with the states having a lot of power.

Federalist Party The party of George Washington and John Adams, which believed in a strong federal government.

free state A state of the Union which abolished slavery and allowed people who have been slaves to be free.

French Revolution An uprising that broke out in France in 1789 and got rid of the royal family. The revolutionaries set up a republic in 1792.

Gadsden Purchase U.S. purchase of territory from Mexico that opened a route for a southern railroad.

Great Depression The worst U.S. economic depression, which happened in the 1930s.

House of Representatives The lower House of Congress. Each state is represented in the House according to its population. Representatives are elected every two years.

House Un-American Activities Committee (HUAC) A committee that investigated activities by Communists and others who were thought to be anti-American. The investigation lasted from the 1930s until 1975.

impeachment A way of removing a president from office for wrongdoing. The House of Representatives hears the case and recommends impeachment to the Senate, which makes the decision on whether to keep the president. A two-thirds majority is needed to remove the president from office.

inauguration The official ceremony held when the new president and vice president take office.

Independent A politician who does not belong to any political party.

inflation A rise in prices for goods and services.

interventionist Someone who believes governments should get fully involved in another country's economy or society to change it.

judiciary The judges, lawyers, and court system that organize the U.S. laws.

kitchen cabinet A cabinet made of the president's friends.

landslide An overwhelming victory, either in votes at an election or in seats in Congress.

League of Nations An international group formed after World War I to stop future wars.

legislature A group of elected people who make laws. The U.S. legislature is the Congress.

Louisiana Purchase An area of land west of the Mississippi River that the United States bought from France in 1803.

majority leader The leader of the biggest political party in either house of Congress.

militia A group of civilians who carry arms and fight if there is a national emergency.

minimum wage The lowest salary that an employer can legally pay a worker.

minority leader The leader of the opposition, or smaller, party in the Congress.

Missouri Compromise See page 19.

Monroe Doctrine See page 19.

motion A formal proposal that is discussed and voted on in a debate or a meeting.

national debt The money a government borrows from banks and other countries to pay for running the country.

New Deal The name of Franklin Roosevelt's package of financial and economic reforms of 1933. See page 71.

Nobel Peace Prize An annual prize given to the person who has worked most for world peace. Alfred Nobel, a Swedish chemist who invented dynamite, set it up.

North Atlantic Treaty Organization (NATO) A group of western European and North American countries set up to protect each of its members from attack by the Soviet Union.

patronage A political or administrative job given to a person to gain their support.

political machine See state machine.

progressive candidate Someone who believes in major reform, or changes, within a country, which will have far-reaching effects on its citizens.

racial discrimination The unfair and unequal treatment of one group of people by another based on the color of their skin or their ethnic background.

Reconstruction The program of reform and rebuilding of the southern states at the end of the Civil War. See page 43.

reform A change or changes in government policy, usually of benefit to a country's citizens.

republic A country like the United States governed by an elected head of state called a president.

Republican A supporter of the Republican Party.

Republican Party A political party formed in 1854 by a group of Whigs and Democrats who were against slavery. Abraham Lincoln was its first president. It is one of the two big U.S. political parties today.

Revolutionary War The war between the thirteen American colonies and their British rulers from 1775 to 1783, which led to U.S. independence.

running mate The person chosen by a presidential candidate to campaign for the office of vice president.

secession When one state or part of a country declares its independence from the rest of the country, as the Confederacy did when it left the Union in 1861.

secretary of commerce The U.S. cabinet member responsible for business affairs and trade.

secretary of state The U.S. cabinet member responsible for relations with other countries.

segregation A legal policy to separate different ethnic groups. This law was used in the South before the Civil War to keep African American and white U.S. citizens apart.

Seminole Nation Native Americans who live in Florida.

Senate The upper house of Congress, made up of two senators or representatives from each state. It has 100 members. See also state assembly.

senator A member of the Senate.

slavery Owning people against their will so they have no freedom or civil rights.

solicitor general A senior legal officer of the government just below the attorney general.

state assembly The lawmaking body of an individual state. Forty-nine out of fifty states have a state assembly similar to Congress.

state machine A strong political party that uses its large membership and good organization to control a city, state, or national government of a country. See page 24.

state senate See state assembly.

Supreme Court The highest U.S. court, which decides major constitutional cases. Its chief justice and eight other judges are appointed by the president and approved by the Senate.

tariff A tax on goods imported from other countries. Tariffs are meant to reduce the number of goods bought from overseas by encouraging people to buy home-grown products.

tax A payment that the government collects from individual people or companies. Workers' salaries, companies' profits, and some goods are taxed.

trade union An organized group of workers that protects their rights and fights for better working conditions or pay.

treaty A formal agreement between two or more countries.

truce An agreement, usually temporary, between two or more countries or armies to stop fighting.

two-party political system A political system, such as in America, where two political parties dominate politics.

Union The fifty U.S. states.

vice president The deputy to the president who takes over if he resigns or dies. The first three vice presidents were the runners-up in the presidential election, but he or she is now the president's running mate and a member of the his party, though the presidential candidate and convention may name a running mate of any party.

welfare A system of financial and other assistance set up by governments for people in need.

Whig Party A political party set up to oppose the Democratic Party. It elected its first president, William Harrison, in 1840. The party split up over the subject of slavery and many of its members joined the Democrats or the Republicans in the 1850s.

INDEX